Boy on the Run

Matt Gutbrod

Boy on the Run

Copyright © 2012 by Matt Gutbrod

ISBN: 978-1-57074-059-6

Scripture references are from the following sources: The Holy Bible, New International Version®, NIV®, copyright © 1973, 1978, 1984, 2011 by Biblica, Inc.™. Used by permission of Zondervan. All rights reserved worldwide. The Holy Bible, New Living Translation (NLT), copyright © 1996, 2004, 2007 by Tyndale House Foundation. Used by permission of Tyndale House Publishers, Inc., Carol Stream, Illinois 60188. All rights reserved.

Contents

Foreword

If God ever tells you to take a train ride . . . get ready for the ride of your life! Matt Gutbrod found this out while seeking God. Simply put, he was told to write the story of his own life. Boy on the Run draws the reader into a world of abuse and suffering. Be prepared for gut wrenching honesty as Matt allows us the privilege of traversing his journey from pain and alcoholism to God's provision. The book's earthy transparency looks at a life changed by the power and grace of God.

The Bible tells of similar calls to leave one's home at God's direction. Abram was compelled to leave Ur to travel the deserts in search of Canaan. Fishermen were called from their nets to "fish for men." A prominent Rabbi was led to a life of suffering for the Savior. Similarly, Matt's obedience to take a train ride led to his getting in touch with horrendous childhood abuse. I can see this book finding its way to AA meetings, church gatherings, and college classrooms. I intend to recommend it often to those in search of an authentic encounter with God.

Donald A. Lichi, Ph.D.
Psychologist
Vice-President
EMERGE Counseling Services

As the father of a son who was sexually molested by a family "friend," I felt Matt's pain from a parent's perspective. Read this book and you will better understand the pain, the withdrawal, and the anger that a child goes through who is molested. Know that there is real hope of healing through God's revealing love and truth.

Anonymous father

This book was instrumental in helping me to learn and see that God is sovereign and actively involved in all of the events of our lives. He is not a spectator. Matt's book was a great reminder that no matter how much we run, God will always pursue us.

Anonymous addict

Author's Note

I apologize for some of the language in this book. It was necessary at times to clearly define the horror and depth of the abuse.

The Boy

Preface
Boy on a Train

In preparation for writing this book God whispered in my ear that I should board a train and travel to Seattle, Washington. I was sure that I had misheard my Master's voice. I thought the best thing to do would be to pray about this strange request and try in my human weakness to avoid personal inconvenience at all cost.

I know that since I started trying in earnest to have a relationship with God back in 2000, He had put people in my path who could help me and whom I might be able to help. I am also convinced that He had others in place, but due to my short spiritual attention span, I had completely missed or flat-out ignored them. I knew that I needed to stop missing His callings and pay much closer attention to His will.

As a few days passed, the message remained and my stubbornness fought it tooth and nail. Why was it that God wanted me to take a train to Seattle? I had no connection to the city or the state or much in between here and there. I had started and stopped writing a potential book, but the lack of traction had led me to believe that maybe the timing or the author wasn't right. Was He calling me to get going on this oft delayed book?

As is often the case when my Lord cannot reach me due to human interference, He calls upon my loving wife, Victoria, to reach out to me on His behalf. One night while we were lying in bed she looked over at me and said, "I believe that God has asked you to share something with me, do you have something to tell me?" I smiled, and without any hesitation I said, "He wants me to take a train to Seattle."

Being the practical woman she is, she said, "Did He say when you are supposed to leave?" I knew at that point that things were starting to move in a westerly direction. I said that I didn't have any other information at this point and that I was sure that God would fill me in when it was appropriate.

I had recently been led back into contact with a very godly man named Bill who I had recently talked to after morning Mass. God showed me mercy and led me to ask Bill if he had time for coffee after Mass, which of course he did. Bill and I had coffee and talked about his son whose life resembled my life with the many trials I had endured and sounded a lot like my story. He told me that he had tried for years to help his son, but he had failed.

I asked Bill in the middle of our second coffee meeting if God had ever asked Him to do something that on the surface seemed odd. He knew what I was talking about and he said that yes, God had called him to a certain course of action and he had failed to comply. I could tell that the very thought caused him pain. I had not disclosed God's request of me at that point. He then said, "Remember, Matt, that God spoke to Mother Theresa on a train."

I was awestruck, and I said, "How do I know if the calling is accurate?" He said that I should pray over it, which I had been doing each day at morning Mass for several days. Then he said I should talk about it with my wife, which I had, and I told him these things. He said I should listen closely to God and do as He had asked.

He then said that he would be glad to pay my expenses or our mortgage for the month if that would help. I told him that it wasn't necessary at that point but that I would maybe call on him in the future if the need arose.

Bill promised daily prayers in support of my journey and wanted to know if I would call him along the way. I told him we would talk when I was away, and I very much appreciated his prayers and spiritual support. God's ways are mysterious to me, but I did not see a lot of need to delay my trip any longer. I looked at Bill at the end of our time together, and the Holy Spirit took over at that moment. I believe that God had put Bill and me together as a timely source of fellowship, hope, and the sharing of wisdom that only the Lord can sponsor. I was there to be a beacon of hope for Bill, to let him know that, though his son was struggling mightily, I had recovered from some of the same illnesses and his son would also recover. I said that I believed without a doubt his son would be healed, and there were tears in his eyes when he said, "I hope so."

I told my wife about my conversation with Bill, and later that evening I booked a one-way coach seat on a sixty-hour train ride to Seattle. I was to leave in four days, and I told her that I did not know any other details other than I was to pack light and bring my Bible and remain open to God's further instructions. My wife gave me loving support, and I believe the Holy Spirit was on fire inside her heart as she simply said that I should get going and asked what she could do to help.

I knew that I was going west, and I was at peace with this decision. I called my daughter and asked if she had a few minutes to talk, and she lovingly came over quickly. I told her that I was going on a trip with the Lord, and she smiled and asked where I was going. I said, "Seattle by train," and she shook her head and seemed to be at peace with this as well.

My wife drove me to the Cleveland train station at 1:00 a.m. on a Saturday night and kissed me good-bye. At 3:50 a.m.

I was bound for Chicago with a bad cough that I had had for two weeks and a small bag of clothes, my Bible, my laptop, and a book that my wife had just happened to be reading entitled, The Day Christ Died, by Jim Bishop.

I had been on a train a few times but certainly not for a sixty-hour trip across the country. I got on the train and took my seat, and the noise and crowded seats and rows made me start to wonder if, in fact, I had missed God's message all together. Maybe He meant that I should take a train to Elyria or Toledo which were just a couple of hours away. That seemed like a more reasonable request. He certainly was not going to put me in the middle of this madness for sixty hours. God is funny! As it turns out, the connecting train to Seattle from Chicago was cancelled due to the Red River in North Dakota spilling over the tracks, and after I had completed the eight-hour ride to Chicago, I was, in fact, stranded.

His humor is also a mystery to me, and I found myself in a Starbucks on a Sunday morning trying to find accommodations for the night. I also spoke with Amtrak, and they informed me that there wasn't going to be train service to Seattle until Tuesday. I actually needed two nights of accommodations in Chicago and a wake-up call for Tuesday morning so that I could resume my journey to the Great Northwest.

I spent the day reading The Day Christ Died and writing this Preface of the book. I had titled the book Boy on the Run because I realized that one common theme that came up whenever I thought about my youth and adulthood was that I was always running from and to something that mostly left me longing for more movement and hoping that peace would find me. I went to morning Mass on Monday and spent the rest of the day reading and writing and searching for continued updates from the Lord.

I know that my mind does not work like the well-oiled machine God had originally given me. Despite that fact, when I wait patiently for God to move me in the direction of His will for my life, things have a wonderful way of working out. This is in spite of the clearly proven fact that I am often in haste to move as my will dictates, and in my compulsive manner, that has seldom delivered the desired results. My brain may not be working as planned, but the shell around it is thicker than ever.

Tuesday morning came and off I went to Union Station in downtown Chicago. The journey took a new twist when I was informed by the fine folks at Amtrak that the train to Seattle was cancelled and I had really only two choices at least in their opinion—a trip back to Cleveland and a refund on my ticket or a new ticket to Seattle via Los Angeles. I was committed to somehow, someway getting to Seattle, and this was strength and inspiration from my Lord, I was sure.

I further saw God's hand when Amtrak said that they were sorry, and to make it up to me they were going to give me a sleeper car for the trip to LA. This turned out to be a real blessing, because sitting in a coach seat for forty or fifty hours would probably be too much for this weak soldier. God knows our every need, and He was preparing me for some quality time with Him, and He needed me to be rested and alert if it was going to be productive.

The trip to Los Angeles was spent in prayer, reading the amazing book about Christ's last day on earth, and an incredible exercise in reliving some of the varied days of my youth. This included my many struggles and the paths that the abuse I had suffered led me on. It also thankfully included remembering how all of this eventually led me to the cross and to a decade of healing and a growing love for my merciful Lord.

As the train clicked along, I thought about the little boy I had been, as evil approached and crested through me like a shockingly cold ocean wave. I set out to find him and bring him into focus.

Acknowledgments

This book would never have been possible without the mercy and love of the Lord Jesus Christ. He saved a boy from ruin, and He then put wonderful people in my life so that I could find my voice and sing His praises.

I was shown unconditional love by my daughter, Olivia. In the darkest days she stood beside me and her love has never wavered . . . what a treasure.

When it was time, God brought beauty and wisdom to me when I was introduced to my wife, Victoria. Her support and love have been so needed and so wonderful . . . what a blessing.

In His infinite wisdom God has always brought godly people forward when I was ready. My healing journey made great strides due to the tender counseling provided by Kim and Mary. They showed compassion for the boy I was and helped me move toward the man God intended me to be . . . what insight.

I cannot forget my two sisters, Marie and Nora, who despite my woundedness, fed me and loved me and loved Olivia when we were so needy . . . what a crazy pair.

Thanks to Patti for editing my book with a loving and thoughtful touch. It is apparent you know the Savior . . . what direction.

And finally, I must always be grateful for the many brothers and sisters in AA who have shown me the way to a sober life one day at a time, one meeting at a time, one step at a time, and for that I am eternally thankful. I promise to remember my disease is cunning, baffling, and powerful, and I am always one drink away from resumed misery and one phone call away from not taking that drink . . . what a new life!

God, How Great Thou Art!

Introduction
Running for Cover

I was molested as a small boy. It lasted for several years. I eventually found drugs and alcohol to numb the pain and then based many of my most important life decisions on my anger, my depression, and my need to survive.

I was suffering from PTSD (Post Traumatic Stress Disorder). It was calamitous on its best day. I created havoc that created havoc that created havoc even when I fully understood that I was simply repeating the same behavior day in and day out and very much expecting a different outcome.

The little boy inside of me, who was so badly hurt when he was just seven years old, never got the chance to grow and mature and become a man. I simply withered and became a shell of the divine design that God intended. I became a man only in height and weight and chronological age but not in the ways that matter, the ones that would have allowed me to have a sense of normalcy inside my own skin and the ways that would have allowed me to make healthy choices and lead a productive life.

So many men who were molested as boys by other males, who found alcohol and drugs and other things that allowed them to cope with feelings of guilt and shame, and who lacked a voice, are still living, or at least breathing, in pain, anger, and dysfunction.

Their families and friends have stopped being able to help, and lives are ruined and relationships destroyed. God's plan to heal the abused child inside is wiped away by their daily detrimental choices. These are choices we make to remain in the misery that victims of childhood sexual abuse experienced at the hands of trusted family or church members or neighbors, and unfortunately, many can really relate to this.

I am here to tell you in my most limited but God inspired way that you do not have to live in hell anymore. There are people who can help and loved ones who want to step into the void for you, and all you have to do is say these simple words: "God, I am in so much pain, please help me."

Do this on your knees and then reach out to the people who have been all around you without you even realizing it. Ask them to help you, and you will start the healing process. The road to healing is difficult, but it is worth it. God's hand is extended at this very moment, and all He needs is for you to be open to His voice.

I found Alcoholics Anonymous (AA) the right place for me to start. It not only helped me stop drinking, but the 12-Step Program was very helpful in my understanding of my powerlessness and how God's grace could change me.

You will find God's angels on earth as I did in AA meeting halls and counselors and friends who want to help. The light will grow and, if you stick with it long enough, God may ask you as He did me to take a trip with Him. He may put you in front of a computer and ask you to write some things down that He would like you to share with men who have similar histories and who want so badly to find some peace.

He will take you places that will bring you wisdom and hope and show you things that will help you understand, and you will change and begin to find that elusive peace. Someday in the future He may tap you on the shoulder and say, "I want you to go hug that total stranger or give that beggar whatever you can spare." He may even ask you to risk your life and speak the truth to others and not to worry about the consequences.

He may put you on a train and tell you to get to work and you will have the chance to obey Him, and I recommend you do so. He will change you, and He will build on your strengths to further His kingdom on earth. Try in your limited human way to do what He asks of you and continue to be open to His voice, come what may.

But let's not get ahead of ourselves. Let me first give form and shape to the evil and the ghost that I had become so that hopefully some man out there will say, "Yeah, that's how I felt." I can relate because no matter what God's divine mercy can accomplish (and it is beyond our comprehension), the abuse that has stolen young boys' lives is real. The secrets are carried on from generation to generation, and victims get re-victimized by people in their lives who do not want the darkness removed or who simply can't handle the truth.

They may want to leave sleeping dogs alone and go on about their lives and maintain their often forgotten or blocked memories. In my situation the incest and continued molestation was like a grenade going off in the middle of the house, and to this day there are family members who deny the grenade's existence and its long-lasting effects. One of my siblings simply revised history and said that these events happened after he had left the house for good even though he was fourteen or fifteen years old and right in the middle of it.

And it's vital that we never lose sight of the predator in our midst who takes innocents and leads them into privatized hell where the child is subjected to unbelievable cruelties and starts down the path of confusion, self hatred, addiction, and often premature death by suicide or other outcomes that simply aren't acceptable.

The evil that I am speaking of is of the deepest and darkest nature. The predators that take children and abuse them for their own sadistic satisfaction have broken away from all moral form. Their sick minds rule their lives, and their fantasies and hateful needs often leave children in their path at great risk.

I believe that the person who violated me was himself ruined at the hands of a trusted member of our church. I am always intrigued as to the origin of my particular abuse—meaning who was the original abuser who started the chain of events that led to the malicious actions of my perpetrator.

That person has the blood of many ruined lives on their head, and I am confident that there is a special place in hell for their actions. The other individuals who may be held accountable by God are those bystanders who for some reason witnessed these heinous acts and they either turned a blind eye or gave the abuser their consent in exchange for future considerations.

I have heard of parents turning a blind eye as spouses and grandparents abused their own children and they felt powerless to stop these acts. I know there will be excuses made for some weak individuals and some will deny ever being a witness, but God will sort that out in time. If they have a conscience, the least they can do is apologize and seek a full confession for sins of omission and commission.

I know of adult males who are lost in a state of shame and guilt, and they have left their homes and families and now live in single rooms or they live nomadically in shelters or on the streets.

They have not been able to make a healing connection with God and have often turned to alcohol and drugs and escapism due in large part to their shame and guilt and self loathing. That may be due to the abuse but also to their lost abilities to make good decisions, where life's harsh realities have only added to this feeling of worthlessness and shame.

Men in our society are expected to be strong and fearless and be the provider for themselves and their families. They are to avoid showing weakness in every aspect of life. These expectations rule our existences much like giving birth and being a mother may rule many women's lives.

As I was growing up in the 1960s and 1970s, these roles were the norm in most of the homes that I visited, and they were depicted strongly on television and movies. Being a strong, heterosexual male and a successful provider who brought home the bacon and defended the family home was the model existence.

My father survived the Great Depression as a child, fought in The Big One, World War II, and was given a Purple Heart for being wounded in action and a Bronze Star for valor. He raised eight children and seldom missed a day of work. That was the model that I was to follow, and it was deeply imbedded in the very essence of who I was and how I evaluated myself as a boy and as a man.

Homosexuality was wrong and it was sinful and it was the very opposite of what I wanted to be. When I was molested by another male, my young mind could not comprehend what that meant. It left me in a state of insane confusion without anyone to talk to and no place to turn.

My abuser was in my life on a regular basis, and he was threatening me and continuing to sexually abuse me and drive me deeper and deeper into a darkness that would become my day-to-day existence for many years to come.

My abuser died in 1995 and the day of the funeral I drank and cried and laughed and was completely out of my mind. He was gone and that was good, but I never had the ultimate courage to confront him. That left me feeling hollow and angry and worn out, and those feelings lasted a very long time. A time that I would like very much to forget but also a time when I started to come face-to-face with my own life, my own death, and a decision that would change my life forever.

That decision was to get sober. It took me several years to find the right path, which was the path illuminated by God. I struggled to do it my way, but He finally got my attention, I finally recognized the people that He was putting in my way, and I stayed sober.

That path has led me to a new life filled with blessings that I would not have had if I had kept drinking. It led me to a better relationship with my daughter which is so very precious to me today. The path led me to a loving wife who walks beside me and is the salve for my many rough spots and who shows me God's love on earth.

This God-designed path has led me to new ways of healing, especially to EMDR Therapy and its miraculous healing powers. (EMDR Therapy is Eye Movement Desensitization and Reprocessing. It is an integrative psychotherapy approach that has been extensively researched and proven effective for the treatment of trauma through the use of a set of standardized protocols. Please see Chapter 11 and the Appendix at the end of this book for more detailed information). The fact that I am writing this book is a true testament to how far God has brought me over the last twelve plus years. It is a miraculous journey that I want to share.

The days I spend on God's path hold promise and value. His ways are always leading me to healing and light and a new life. I hope that if your journey has begun, you stay the course and allow God's mercy to heal you and bring you peace.

If you are still in darkness and feeling lost and in need of hope, as I said earlier, simply get on your knees and pray a simple prayer, and then reach out to someone who can help you and start your healing walk today.

The rest of this book is my story. A life redeemed by Christ. A life that was cast into darkness by hideous and sinful acts but that has been brought into God's great light. For His love and mercy I will be forever thankful.

My hope is that those injured boys who live in darkness as men may find God's path to healing and may in some small way be inspired by the telling of my story and my return to the light! I believe that God has led me to this divine appointment as a way of further healing me and as a way to reach other men and maybe their loved ones with a message of hope.

God has a divine plan, and He stays the course that will always lead to redemption if we accept His will for our lives. The road back from childhood abuse can be very difficult, and my journey is a testament to that. However, carrying these horrors alone for a lifetime is not a life. Living with PTSD for a lifetime is not living. Missing out on life's joyful moments due to addiction and isolation is a great tragedy.

None of the victims of childhood sexual abuse deserved to be abused. They were innocent and no matter how others, including family members, try to bury the past, God will bring the truth to light and redeem the innocent either on earth or in heaven.

I am hopeful that my story will bring some of the light to this darkness. God has redeemed me and continues to lead me away from the misery and toward an eternity with Him. I hope you will book your ticket on the train to redemption and salvation and stop the self destructive path that you may be on.

I know what it is like to be a boy on the run from misery

and fear. I know what it is like to lose trust and hope. I know what it is like to be alone and close to the end. But more importantly I know what God's wondrous mercy and love feel like, and I am sure that there is no coincidence that you are reading this book. Please keep an open mind, and He will never let you down! You can do this, and God will help!

I Need a New Christ

I need a new Christ
A new Savior in glorious color
Painting over my pain with new light
Changing my walls to windows
My loneliness to unification
With a gentle brushstroke
My sins, my sins are covered
By the kindest King
In pastel perfection my horrors redeemed
I want to know Him . . . need to know Him
In merciful heavenly blues
And bright gentle yellows
Redone in sun burnt orange
A warm glow forever felt
Changing my now to eternity
A brand new shade of saved.

Chapter 1
A Boy on the Run to Baseball

After the first series of attacks, I turned inward and was living most of the time in my head and on constant alert. It was around this time that I fell in love with baseball and baseball cards. I really looked forward to that first spring Sunday when we would stop on the way home from church at the pharmacy, and there they were—that first box of baseball cards for the new season.

My eyes would just gravitate toward and stare at the new season's packaging and the box that must have contained fifty individual packs of cards. I wanted to take the whole box home but I was usually limited to one or maybe two packs. I can still smell the gum and feel the crisp cards and the shiny faces of each player.

I would tear open that first pack of cards and before we made it home I was well on my way to knowing the players and the final statistics from their prior seasons. I knew their height, weight, their hometown, which hand they threw with, and which side of the plate they batted from. I really devoured every bit of potential information available on each and every card that came my way. The highlight of a summer day was riding my bike to the pharmacy and for two thin dimes getting two packs of cards that included ten cards per pack and one stick of bubble gum in each.

The bubblegum was sometimes as hard as a rock but that didn't matter. I would lick the fine white powder off the gum and pop it in my mouth, and slowly but surely the gum would soften. I would then drop my bike on the sidewalk out front and tear into the first pack of cards hoping for a Cleveland Indians player or a big name star. I just hoped that they weren't doubles. Doubles were cards that a collector already had.

Topps, the big card company, would space out the big stars throughout the season, and so if you bought a lot of individual packs of cards in a short period of time, the chances of getting doubles was good. Two packs of doubles could really ruin the bike ride home. On the other hand, two packs of new cards including a couple of big names could turn a whole day around, and for just a short span of time I could almost forget that I had to go home and that he was there and that this perfect moment could be shattered in a heartbeat.

It was like that with almost every moment that held any enjoyment during these terrible years of my life. I was on edge and anxious regardless of where I was. My ability to trust anyone was destroyed. It left me in a crazy state of agitation most of the time. The simple moments in my young life evaporated like wisps of smoke, and I just wasn't able to go back and relive them.

There was a demarcation line in time that clearly indicated the days before the first attack and after. There was no going back, the future was going to be really ugly, and I did not know how long I would feel this way. I pleaded inside my own head for someone to come and save me

I could peddle that bike as slowly as it would go without falling over just to prolong the inevitable. The whole experience brought me some much needed escape, and it was such a solitary experience that it still puts a smile on my face. Once I got home my mind shifted gears and I was on alert. If I found out he was not home, I would go to my room and once again pour over each aspect of the new cards and start to sort them into their individual teams.

I had this ritual, which irked some of my siblings, but only a kid in my situation would really understand. My imagination was my way out of feeling horrible. The landing at the stairs leading to the second floor and the five bedrooms was large and it allowed me to sit on the top step and arrange a sizeable baseball field with my cards. I would then orchestrate a complete game including the play-by-play in my own field of dreams.

I could have my hometown Indians beat the crap out of the vaunted Tigers any time I wanted, and that was pure fantasy. I could play American League teams versus National League teams long before anyone ever heard of inter-league play. I was the Commissioner, the Manager, and the Players, and I was free to do as I pleased.

The league was mine to run, and the players answered to me, and if they got out of line they stayed in the box and would not see the light of day for a long while. As my life spiraled out of control, the one thing I could control and enjoy was the field at the top of the stairs

I was especially fond of the African-American players. Willie Mays and Hank Aaron were legends who were in the National League. I seldom got to see them play, so they were regulars at the ballpark at the top of the stairs. They would hit titanic home runs and make implausible defensive plays, and no one could stop them. Well almost no one.

The truth was that I was in the middle of the upstairs foot traffic from bedroom to bedroom and bedroom to bathroom, and of course I was blocking the stairway up and down. My siblings sometimes just had had enough and they would light into me and kick some cards around and complain to my parents but very little would happen, unless of course it involved him.

If he had any opportunity to destroy the setting, he took immense pleasure in kicking the cards down the hall or grabbing a handful and tearing them apart and leaving me in misery and the game halted due to my growing sense of darkness. He knew the exact acts of cruelty that would break my spirit and send me insanely under a bed or in a closet or down into the basement, any place where I might be safe from any physical or sexual attack.

I used to listen to a lot of games on the radio, and I would imitate the announcers and give the game a real sense of drama and reality. I also could watch his bedroom door and the front door to monitor his comings and goings and be prepared to bust a move if necessary.

I would be oblivious to every other thing going on around me except for my game and those two doors. If I heard his voice coming towards the steps I would shove the cards off to the side and dart into the bathroom and lock the door.

I would then slide the drawer out so that even though he could pick the lock, he could only open the door about two inches before it rammed into the drawer. He would do this, and then he would stare at me through the large bathroom mirror and whisper, "I am waiting, asshole," or "Open this fucking door, asshole," or my favorite, "I will give you three seconds to come out and then I am going to kick your ass." Yeah like I was going to make that ridiculous move and open that door to the big bad wolf.

He caught me one time when I slipped trying to make it in the bathroom and he shoved me inside and started to kick the shit out of me. Then he locked the door and pulled out the drawer and the horror really began. He actually caught me in the bathroom a couple of times and did a number on me. It was almost forty years after those horrible memories before I actually allowed another human being in the bathroom with me.

Somehow, I could be fully involved in my card collection learning where players were born, their lifetime batting averages, the minor league teams that they had played for, and at the same time I was ever watchful for attacks or warning signs. Ultimately, this became my existence, especially in the summer months when there was no school to hide in and the days were long and my vigilance in full force.

There was no end to my hyper vigilance. That was front and center throughout my day. I kept careful watch for the movements of my attacker, and my eyes and ears became finely tuned to his whereabouts and his habits. To be left alone with him was scarier than any horror movie I have ever watched. My skin would crawl and my hands would sweat and I would immediately begin to think of places to hide depending on his exact location at that moment. If he was upstairs, I would have access to the outdoors as well as the crawl space in the basement. If he was on the main floor, I had the locked bathroom or the attic, at least until the day he found me in the attic.

The attic locked from the outside so you were careful not to let anyone know you were up there, especially not him. One day while I was home with a few of my siblings, I found refuge in the attic with a handful of baseball cards to keep me occupied. I must have made a loud noise and he heard me. He came to the attic door and opened it and started asking who was up there. This was an unfinished attic with rafters and insulation and some boxes stored on plywood.

The only place to hide was on the insulation in between

the wooden framing. Believe me, that was not a comfortable spot. It was made worse that day because it was warm out, and the heat would rise and drive most sane people out of the close confines of the attic. I was not sane, so the rising heat was not my first concern. It was then that I heard him start to climb into the doorway that led to the hard wooden steps up into the main room of the attic.

I moved as far back into the recesses of the A-frame structure as I could and was barely able to keep from screaming bloody murder when I saw his face looking for me, scanning the minimal places I could be. Then his eyes met mine, and he said, "Hey asshole, what ya hiding for?" I said nothing. I was frozen and too afraid to breathe. He then said, "Hey asshole, you better come out here because at the count of three I'm gonna lock you in here forever." When I didn't move, he made a lunge towards me and my heart leaped into my throat and I moved even further into the attic.

He just laughed at my craziness. He said, "Okay asshole, you're going to fry up here, and no one is going to find you. I am going to be waiting for you down here just in case." I was doomed. He had me trapped, and there was no place for me to go. Tears ran down my face, and the cards I had in my hand were ruined, and I threw the worst of them against the wall in a rage.

I then heard the lock being moved into place and I knew that I was in big trouble. My little boy brain was really struggling to figure out what to do next. I sat and waited and sweated and worried that someone would find me dead up there.

I began to read the back of one of the cards and then another and slowly my heart stopped racing, and I let my imagination run as I tried to recite entire starting lineups for teams. This consisted mostly of the American League teams because that was where my beloved Indians resided. I could name the great Detroit Tigers with Kaline, Horton, Stanley, Northrup, their great catcher Bill Freehan, and their ace Denny McLain. That was a heck of a team. I always wanted the Indians to have a team like that. They cleaned the Indians' clocks just about every time the two teams played.

Somehow my mind was swept away from the horrific menace waiting for me at the bottom of the steps, and I was running down the various lineups and reading the small paragraphs about each player and reviewing the math of their batting averages. I have no idea how long I was lost in my diamond shaped head.

I then heard a voice from the doorway below and it was my mom who had unlocked the door asking if I was up there. I started to cry tears of joy, and I said, "Yes," and she said to come down. I knew I might be in trouble, but who cared at that point. At least I wasn't going to die a horrible, sweaty death.

When I got to the bottom of the steps, she was deeply concerned and she held me and wiped sweat from my face with her apron and asked what I was doing up there. I just cried, and she made me promise I would never go up there again. Then she looked at me and said, "Who locked you in?" It was one of many opportunities that I had to get help, but the fear of him finding out just silenced me, and I just shrugged. That was the end of my hiding in the attic. I would just have to run faster and find new places to run to.

Baseball and card collecting were refuges for me. So much of my life at this time was spent inside my head. I grew up in a large and loud house that was only really at peace late at night. The rest of the time was constant movement and people coming and going and televisions and arguments and battles for property or space or solitude or food or bathrooms or bikes or so many things that were shared by ten people.

The family was really an outgoing sports oriented group that had its hub in a five-bedroom home and its spiritual and educational base at St. Bridget's Catholic Church and School. My father had a half-court, cement basketball court installed in the backyard which became a neighborhood hangout and the center of many hotly contested hoops games. The most hotly contested and the ones that often ended in either physical or emotional injury were the games played against other siblings.

I had four brothers who were all very competitive and three sisters who were competitive as well, and it was usually the younger kids in groups of twos or threes playing against one or two of the older kids. We played from very early spring, sometimes in gloves, until late into early winter.

There was usually one decent basketball and then two or three others that were in some state of deflation, and they were the warm up balls. Before the abuse started, one of the worst days of my young life was when I had the court to myself and I could not find the good ball. I was as deflated as the basketball I was using. There is nothing worse than hitting a fifteen foot jumper and having the ball lie flat under the hoop. It was hard to get excited about the practice session at that point. Basketball really became my favorite game to play.

My first memorable experience on a baseball field, other than T-ball, was in the fourth grade. It was late spring. School would be out soon, and my Mother had signed us up for various levels of baseball depending on our ages. The first practice I went to we were each given a couple of at bats to see what we could do. The coach was the pitcher.

The first time up I grounded out to his son at shortstop. The second time up the coach hit me in the ribs with a pitch and as I lay in the dirt trying to catch my elusive breath, I thought maybe baseball was better played at home in the yard with kids pitching. I finished the year and was never really very aggressive at the plate. I played one more season, but then decided I had had enough of organized baseball.

Any sport, but especially basketball, baseball, and football, was my great escape. It did not matter whether the games where being broadcast on television, the radio, live at the enormous Cleveland Municipal Stadium, the old Cleveland Arena, or the newly built Cleveland Coliseum, or the games that I participated in, sports ruled my life and were always a central focus of our family life.

When I was in great pain, I found and ran to sports. When I was incapable of dealing with the weight of my problems, I went to sports as my sanctuary. It was what I knew and what I loved, and I had a great hunger for statistics and stories and for my favorite Cleveland teams to win so that I could feel proud to be from Cleveland. I was a kid with a secret, a damning secret that kept me from most of the true joys going on around me — except for my love of sports.

As time passed and I got bigger, we had some tackle football games with the bigger kids in the neighborhood. I was as skinny as a rail, but I realized that if he played, I could possibly enact some revenge. That was at least the plan at the beginning of the game. There were a few moments of glory when I got the rare chance to deliver a cheap shot to the gut or to the groin when he was at the bottom of the pile. I paid dearly the next play but what the hell. There weren't many better moments in those days than when I heard him howl in pain and I was the one delivering the blow.

I never wanted to be on his team. He would make sure that I never got the ball, and even though we were teammates he would still take the opportunity to give me a cheap shot whenever possible. There was no real reason for me to be in the offensive huddle so I just stayed flanked out and waited for the chance to pile on when he was on the bottom.

There was one day each summer when football was king and I seldom slept the night before with anticipation. My father was the marketing coordinator for Cleveland Coca-Cola. Each August they had a contest and the winners got to go to Cleveland Browns Training Camp and spend the day with the players. My dad would take my older brother and me, and it was the coolest way for a sports addict like me to spend a summer day. We would get autographs, watch the morning and afternoon practices, and in between we would join the players in the cafeteria for lunch.

I remember watching these giant men eat the biggest plates of food I had ever seen—with ease. I don't remember eating anything because I was just staring and catching glimpses of the stars like Leroy Kelly or Walter Johnson or Frank Ryan that I would cheer on each Sunday that fall. I felt like I was really privileged to be there, and it was often the highlight of my troubled summer.

The trips to Browns camp and to watch the Cleveland Indians play at the vast confines of Municipal Stadium were wonderful memories of safety and peace when I could actually let my guard down and take in all that was going on around me. The Indians were always pretty lousy, but the experience was awesome.

I can still remember walking up the ramp from the main concourse and out to the field. We usually had good seats and I enjoyed all of the sights and smells, but the game was the main attraction. There were no cell phones or other significant entertainment going on like there is today. This was a baseball game and that was enough.

One of the great sounds of my youth was the booming fireworks that would go off anytime the Indians hit a home run. It was one of the few times that I actually liked loud noise. Since that first attack and the onset of PTSD and to this very day, I jump at the sound of loud noises. However, on a beautiful summer night, far from my abuser, the sound of fireworks was music to my sensitive ears.

The love of sports was then and has always been a coping mechanism for the pain and confusion I dealt with on a regular basis. I could leave behind my anxieties and be the boy that I was. A boy who only wanted to fit in and not live in fear and confusion. I wanted to be able to spend an entire day feeling safe and away from my thoughts, and sports could do that. It was my numbing tool up until the day I took my first drink, and even though I have now been sober for many years, I still run to sports when I struggle.

I occasionally think back to those days when I believed that sports stars were playing because they loved the game and my imagination was the greatest sports arena in the world. I could take the games anywhere in my head, especially in hiding places or when I ran into the woods or any place a young boy could run to and be safe. And I was fast because I had to be.

My reality was that my attacker was always just down the road or down the hall or waiting in the shadows to bring me back to a miserable state of being. I was a young boy on the run, and I hoped some day I would end up in a place he would never find me and I could be safe . . . every little boy deserves to be safe, doesn't he?

Chapter 2
God, Based on the Description of a 6-Foot Nun

The stories about nuns get better with age. Like football victories on epic fields in six-below temperatures, they became lore and legend. If we get on the topic, my siblings and I can really "spin it" especially if nieces and nephews are in the room. The nuns get taller and meaner as each year passes.

Growing up in the 60s and 70s in parochial schools there was a certain amount of intimidation that the sisters used when dealing with the unruly and the unkempt. There was no one aware of the abuse or keeping watch over the care of their students as there is today.

Nuns had free reign to bring order to a most chaotic setting, and though weapons were not officially allowed, rulers and pointers and other wooden weapons were. When necessary, some nuns felt they were also well within their "God-given" rights to perform the "grab and shake." The grab and shake, since outlawed by both the World Wrestling Federation as well as the World Wrestling Association, often happened out of nowhere.

You would be messing around in the middle of a line having a great time and getting big laughs when out of the sky a large, well-calloused hand would grab you by the scruff of the neck and lift you and shake you. Then you would be brought to an expansive bosom and inevitably find yourself face-to-face with the world's largest crucifix attached to the world's largest rosary, and your judge and jury were assembled and your case heard and your conviction upheld by the Supreme Court all before the next bell rang. When the extremely one-sided battle came to a close, you were left feeling as though God was very disappointed in you, and you of course were on the shortcut path to the fire and molten lava of hell.

The image I had of God as a young boy was mostly associated with guilt and shame and confusion. He was omnipotent and knew much like Santa Claus when you were bad. He stood in judgment of all of our actions and the reality seemed to be that getting to heaven was not something a goof-off like me was going to be able to attain.

God had the overall image of a taskmaster who suffered for us, and we were supposed to be obedient and repentant. This was associated with behavioral defects both large and small, so there was very little room for minor offenses. I remember hearing rumors about small white lies or venial sins but my search for a list of things that God looked the other way on seemed simply out of my reach.

There was however one place for a terrible little sinner like me to go if I wanted to get cleaned up and that was, drum roll here, the confessional. I remember seeing little seven or eight year olds coming to tears when that first confession drew near. There were stories of small children being dropped into a chute in the floor of the confessional and being sent directly in to hades without the possibility of parole — and that was just for chewing gum or passing objectionable material in classroom notes.

I know that I had a very colorful imagination but when a nun whispered in your ear that you were a little hellion and that you would come to no good end, it did cast a pretty impressive cloud over your self-image especially at the time when writing in cursive was keeping you up at night. My ability to put things in perspective was very limited. It was shape up or start making plans for a mighty warm eternity.

I had some advantages with four older siblings having gone through the gauntlet ahead of me. They seemed to make it home alive each evening, and they were open to discussing certain acts and deeming them hell worthy or not. So I had a pretty good sense of what the really indefensible behavior was, and I fully intended to stay away from those activities.

They also offered a "Who's Who" of nuns that you should avoid if at all possible. They extended that field intelligence by letting me know how to defend myself if in fact I found myself on the wrong side of a certain particular nun. It was important information like, "She's a lefty," or "She has a glass right eye," and other vital survival information that went a long way towards living through grade school and staying out of the eternal flames of damnation.

But I had a more horrific problem than the nuns. I was in the second grade when I was sexually molested for the first time. I am not sure exactly, but I probably weighed 40 or 45 pounds. I was a skinny kid. I was just skin and bones and blond hair and innocence. As I said earlier, I loved sports, especially anything to do with Cleveland sports teams. I loved to collect baseball cards and watch games on television or listen to them on the radio and then go out into the yard and imitate what I had seen and heard.

I was just an American kid growing up during the Cold War. The only thing I really hated was the Soviet Union. I did not know why, other than they were going to bomb us any day now and they were evil and the U.S. were the Good Guys and the color red was bad. Beyond that I knew little.

I had Sister Mary Bryant in the second grade. She was a soft-spoken woman with red hair and freckles and the most unattractive glasses that were available to nuns at that time. She seemed to genuinely like children and me especially because at that time I offered very little rebellion and was a good student. The first half of the school year was uneventful, and time passed and Christmas was great and my life was simple and I slept without interruption each and every night until the day my life changed.

There is a moment in time that must break God's heart, and that is when innocence meets evil and a young life is changed forever. There can never be innocent thoughts again. There is no rewind or redo. There is only the breaking of bonds and trusts, and hell is released and comes to life on earth. The sun hides and the stars fly away and dreams become nightmares. Sleep becomes filled with horrors and all that a little mind can handle is silence and shock and despair.

There isn't a seven-year-old who can comprehend how much their world has been fractured. I knew only that someone I had trusted had hurt me in ways that I did not know existed. I hoped that it would stop and someone would tell me it was just a dream and that when I woke up, I would go off to school and everything would be okay.

My throat hurt from being choked and my butt hurt from being penetrated and I could not think about anything else except: What did I do to cause this? I must be a bad boy and there must be something wrong with me. I was being punished for something, though I had no idea what that could be.

I remember where that first attack took place. I remember how I was still there afterwards and I was frozen in place and I had no expression on my face and all I kept hearing was, "Don't tell anyone or you will die." A few days later the second attack took place and it was similar and I offered little resistance. This time the sexual violation was accompanied by physical abuse and that included a punch that left me gasping and a smack to the head that left me dizzy. Then without warning it was over and there was silence and more silence and then darkness as I closed my eyes and mercifully passed out.

I refused to come to dinner and would not speak to anyone and stayed as quiet as possible even in that loud house. I hoped that if I remained very still and kept my mouth shut, nothing more would happen to me. I no longer cared about anything.

The things that I enjoyed simply went away — their appeal was lost in the confusion of my mind. I spent time hiding under the bed and getting used to breathing in dust and staring blankly at walls for what seemed like endless amounts of time. Those things which would have seemed ridiculous just a few days ago became very tolerable in comparison to what might happen outside of my little tomb.

I shrugged off the consistent questions from my mom and dad asking what was wrong and if I was feeling okay. My mom was checking for fever and worried that I was coming down with something and wondering what she could get me and thinking maybe she should take me to the doctor.

I was oblivious to it all as I mimed my way through the day and went to school and said nothing and went home with the fear that something else was going to happen and it was going to be even worse and I was bad. I was somehow causing this and wondering what was going to happen next.

I would hide and try not to scream because I felt like I was going out of my mind. Was this the end of the world? Was this how I was always going to feel and what was going to happen next and why wasn't someone helping to protect me?

The next time I met my attacker I was not going to let him catch me, so I played dead until his guard was down and then I sprang out of the room and out the door and into the big, wide world hoping that I was fast enough to outrun him. I even asked God to help me be fast. I didn't need the speed that day because my attacker was waiting for me to return. He knew I would, so why should he waste his energy chasing this crazy kid around the neighborhood.

Later that day, as I was shooting baskets alone, my attacker and another male came walking around the side of our house and my entire being went into overload. The hair on my neck stood straight up and I had only one thought . . . run. I ran in the opposite direction and ran directly into the house and dove onto the living room couch. I held on for dear life. I clawed my way as far into that poor couch as I could get. I was not going to leave and I was not going to talk and I was not going to eat and I was not going to ever leave that couch.

I had every bit of strength focused on my grip and I can't remember breathing or how long I was there, and when my mom finally sat down and rubbed the back of my neck, I jumped out of my skin.

I dug my self even deeper and hoped that she was there to save me. She asked if I was alright, and I simply shook my head. She asked if I was hungry, and I shook my head, and then she said that she was going to call the doctor.

That was the first good news that I had gotten in awhile, because I was convinced that between the doctor and my parents someone was going to find out what was going on. I would be saved from more punishment, at least that was what I hoped would happen. I was a wreck, and that little boy was only beginning his descent into hell.

There would be many more horrible days ahead filled with enough anger and physical, mental, and sexual abuse that there would be very little left of little me . . . no more hope and no more joy and no more easy nights

There would be just fear and self loathing and more fear that would last for many years to come. God seemed so far away and distant, and I would spend many years wondering where He was during those dark days. I became angry at God, and I knew I would be going to hell, and very little could change that, and that was final.

After running a battery of tests, our family doctor found the whole situation out of his realm of expertise. I seemed to be having flu-like symptoms but not a flu that he had experience in, so he recommended that I be admitted into the Cleveland Clinic for some additional testing.

The Cleveland Clinic was fast becoming a world-renowned hospital, and he was sure that they would fix me right up. A few days later my parents drove me through downtown Cleveland and up to Cedar Road to the biggest hospital I could imagine. For the first time in many days I was actually excited. I was sure that the doctors would discover something that would be the evidence that my parents needed to stop the madness that was happening to me.

I spent ten days being put through every conceivable test and exam, and I met doctors with accents I had never heard. They each lined up for their crack at the mystery that was my unusual behavior and condition. What would make a small child stop eating and stop talking and stop participating in school and hide under beds and all kinds of weird behavior that just a couple of weeks before did not exist? I felt safe for the first time in weeks. I wanted them to come up with the answers, but they could take their time—I did not want to go home.

The endless battery of tests and conferences delivered very little in the way of a diagnosis and there were some very confused, highly educated men and women who just could not find the cause, and thus the solution, to what was upsetting this small boy.

The last day I was there a new face showed up in my room. He told me he was a different kind of doctor. He was a psychiatrist, whatever that meant. He asked me a series of questions that I refused to answer, and then he moved very close and whispered to me, "Who hurt you, little man? Someone has hurt you, haven't they?"

He knew that I was not suffering from some virus or other but that someone had laid hands on me and that I was probably in some state of shock. This was 1968 and the first wave of soldiers was returning from Viet Nam with some of the same symptoms. These symptoms were called "shell shock" during World War II but they would soon be known as PTSD or Post Traumatic Stress Disorder, which left victims in a catatonic state of shock due to significant trauma.

I was released back into the same situation that I had left with a tentative appointment to be seen by the same psychiatrist I had met. The appointment got moved and then cancelled, and I was given the okay to return to all normal activities as if what I was going through was normal.

My mind raced and my heart skipped and the fear came flooding back and there was not going to be a rescue and all those doctors were not going to be able to help me. I was alone again with my nightmares, just a boy on the run for his life, again.

The abuse resumed again shortly after my return but this

time with a new fervor and some new punishment to be sure that I didn't go off and tell anybody anything again, and believe me I got that message loud and clear. My mouth was sealed, and I was just going to have to find another way to avoid the monster. I was going to have to be faster and find better hiding places and keep moving at all times and somehow remain out of his reach.

I was just a little boy with a big secret and no one to turn to. I was in way over my head, and my mind was just not working the way it used to. I returned to school and to the gentle voice and loving care of Sister Mary Bryant who knew only that I had been very sick and I was better. She assured my parents that she would take very good care of me, and she did.

I sat like a mannequin and made as little noise as possible. When I was called on for answers, I said nothing. When the bell rang, I jumped, and when it was time to get on the bus to go home, I hoped the bus would get lost and drive around in circles, and I would never have to go home again.

The days crept by and there were silences and my attacker was finally leaving me alone. It was better for awhile. The fact that there was no new abuse was a miracle, and I may have actually slept a few nights in a row. But as I guessed, he came back and he threatened me and he made sure that I understood that nothing had changed and that he was going to kill me if I opened my mouth to anyone.

He made sure I understood with some vicious smacks to my head and all the time away melted and the brief time that he lay dormant was a distant memory. My life quickly returned to the foggy, horrible sleepwalk that I knew all too well.

One thing though seemed to change over the next year and that was that my hatred for him grew and my anger started to bubble up and I had dreams of revenge and murder. I was changing and it was not for the best. The evil was being transferred to me. Time passed and the attacks started to be more spaced out. I was getting bigger, and his attention was diverted by other things, including drugs and trouble and self-hatred. His behavior was starting to show up on some peoples' radar screen.

I was not his number one concern anymore. He would still remind me that he was around with some good old-fashioned abuse, but I started to put up a fight and he started getting sloppy and the tide started to change. I was still the boy on the run but I no longer was as frightened by his presence.

I grew smarter, and he was slowly losing interest. The end was not in sight but the war was about to become less one-sided. I didn't know what I was going to do, but I knew that I was going to do something.

Sister Mary Bryant helped me through some very tough times by simply caring and loving me and being a non-threatening ally in the war against my insanity. She has remained one of the few good memories from that time in my life. I look back, and now I know that she was Christ's representative to me.

I would find other Christlike people on my long and winding road back from this hell on earth. But I still have the warm thoughts of Sister Mary Bryant as a replacement for some of the other nuns who seemed to be a bit bitter and crabby. They seemed to lack some much needed compassion because they had no idea what a child was going through at home.

The secret I was carrying around was like a giant stone that I had to carry with me each day of school. They could not know how badly I wanted someone to step forward and hug me and tell me everything was going to be okay. They instead used threats and scolding and way too many references to God's wrath in my estimation. I, on the other hand, did not have a clue about who they were or what they had gone through to make them this crabby.

I learned later in life that God's love was most exemplified by allowing His only Son to be stripped and humiliated, beaten and crucified, all for us and all because He loves us so very much. That was lost on me at the time.

In my opinion the Catholic Church and the Catholic school system did some things very well, and the education prepared us for high school and beyond. I learned about God and forgiveness and about the Saints. However, I did not feel the true essence of God; that being, His tremendous mercy and love, from many of the nuns or the priests whom I encountered.

The priests who preyed on young unsuspecting boys is a great blight on the Church and will be for as long as there are wounded men out there who can't find peace. I believe that someone from our church abused my abuser. He started a chain reaction of sin, pain, and death. Things may have been very different for many lives in our family had that individual been able to control his urges and get the help he needed. I know my life would have been much different.

I would endure more abuse at the hands of my attacker in the late 60s and the beginning of the 70s. I was trying my best to cope with my life and the growing confusion created by PTSD. I fell deeper into the abyss. I also fell deeper in love with sports and collecting baseball and football cards. Though my mind was hyper alert, there were times when sports took me away and gave me a much-needed reprieve from the hell I was going through.

I was on the run and hoping that somehow sports would be my way out. The feelings of fear and shame and pain somehow dissipated when the game started. Thank God the distraction created by sports was there because I am not sure I would have been able to cope without it. Sports may have indeed saved my life!

Chapter 3
Boy Meets Evil

"Ladies and gentlemen, for your boxing entertainment, our main event of the evening is a mixed weight championship fight . . . In the black trunks weighing in at just over two tons with a lifetime record of three million wins and zero losses with over two million knockouts, put your hands together for . . . Evil.

"His opponent this evening in the blue trunks weighing in at ninety pounds soaking wet with a lifetime record of zero wins and dozens of losses, put your hands together for a twelve-year-old boy."

As time passed and my attacker started to get some of his own medicine in the form of my retribution along with his own misery, I began to take on the evil that was being transferred to me one abusive event at a time over the past several years. Starting around the sixth grade I began to act out—picking fights at school and picking on girls and anyone who got in my miserable way.

I could no longer contain the anger that turned sometimes to blind rage. I was losing my ability to stuff it down inside me and swallow hard. The reality was that I was gaining evil confidence as I started to slay the meanest dragon that I would ever face. Though I was able to defend myself against him, I wasn't able to exorcise some of the vast array of demons that he had planted in me.

He was just too big for me to put a hurting on. My counter attacks were annoyances that caused him discomfort, embarrassment, or lost sleep. They were things like running into his bedroom early in the morning and slowly pulling the blankets out from under him, leaving him without blankets and mostly naked and awake and very angry, but usually too hung over to give chase. I also used to open his bedroom door and fire things at his head in rapid order, rousing him. But before he could even realize what was happening, I had left the scene.

I was like the jungle warrior versus the big and highly favored super power. I would not want to stand toe-to-toe and fight it out even in his reduced mental state, because even at this point in time, he would belt me and I would see stars and I would be reminded of my place in the war.

Though I did not realize it, all of the abuse over the last several years had done immense damage to me physically, mentally, psychologically, and emotionally. I was in no-man's-land. I did not know who I was or what I stood for. The core of my being was erased, and it was around this time that my personality started to split, and I needed to deal with the abyss that was my mind and the fast approaching rage in some new way.

I just absolutely could not keep that beast under wraps any longer. As puberty started to set its sights on me and all the crap that goes with that, I was coming apart at the seams, and I was scared and confused beyond my understanding. The only thing to do was to try out some new behavior and see what happened. I was throwing caution to the wind and setting sail on a new and dangerous voyage without compass, nor ship, nor crew. I was just a lost and confused boy looking in the wrong places for acceptance, and it would turn out to be a devastating journey with a price that I was often unable to pay.

I figured that the clown usually got attention so that would be my first new behavioral adjustment. I also thought that the tough kid also got a good amount of attention so I would add that to my repertoire as well. So instead of being a somewhat shy kid and usually no trouble for teachers, I was going to be the complete opposite. The loud obnoxious bully was my first costume choice. I met a man at my father's funeral years later, and he said that we had gone to grade school together and that, quite frankly, he was terrified of me back then. I was caught a little off guard, but then my embarrassment changed to sadness—first for him, and I apologized, and he moved on through the crowd. Then I felt sorry for the little boy I had become and deep sorrow overtook me.

One of the great regrets of the abuse and the aftermath was all those people who didn't know about the abuse and just thought I was an asshole in general. I can never explain what went wrong and why I was the way I was. I started out in life as a gentle, somewhat shy little boy who was polite and cared deeply for his siblings and parents. I came out of the abuse as a shell of that boy, mean on the outside and in complete misery on the inside. Years of living with PTSD will definitely leave you in a most twisted state.

As I rolled out the first hybrid of myself, I found that being the funny bully is not an easy role. Those are generally two distinct roles in the classroom setting, but I was thinking about more of a grand change, so what the heck. I found out pretty early on that you could lose some of the best fans of your comedy act by beating the crap out of them at recess. Nothing turns a true fan into a real mad heckler than an embarrassing beat down right after the lunchtime matinee.

I also was walking on the turf of both the other clowns as well as the self-appointed bullies in the class. Neither found my new approach to their liking, and I soon found out that the bullies were meaner than me and the funny men were funnier. So my act got panned in both arenas, and I had some more bumps and bruises to add to my collection.

I was nothing if I wasn't persistent. I out-performed the clowns with my willingness to do just about anything for a laugh, or at least a groan. Most kids had a sanity line that they just wouldn't or couldn't cross. I, on the other hand, had no known boundaries. If the script called for the grossest, I could do that. If the script called for out-and-out daring, I could do that. If the script called for crude, I could do that as well. I just had more pain and misery to draw from, and I had a desperate need to fit in that the normal run-of-the-mill unmolested kid just couldn't imagine, let alone match.

I remember reading the back of one of my sixth grade report cards a few years back, and the teacher's comments were along the lines of: "Matthew's behavior has changed significantly since last year. Has anything changed at home? Please call the school to discuss."

The bully side of the equation was a little more difficult to master, but I was certainly game. The first kid that I did a number on unfortunately had an older brother who delivered retribution in a quick one-two fashion that left me with a very sore face. I was a little more selective after that. Like most bullies, I picked on the slow and the dumb at first just to build up my reputation.

The tumultuous anger that I had stored just below the surface was a potent tool against just about any opponent. You could hold me down and punch me around, but I would just get angrier. I could draw on the many beat downs I had been through, and eventually the young lad that I was scrapping with would let up and all hell would break loose and the tide would turn in a short moment. He would go from the champ to wishing he had stayed in for recess very quickly.

The problem with this whole new approach to life was that I wasn't making any real friends and the establishment was getting sick and tired of hearing my name on the wrong side of the story every couple of days. I took more than my share of detentions, demerits, notes home, and anything else they could think up to try to get my attention. None of it worked. I was bent out of shape, and no amount of school discipline was going to fix that.

The only thing that saved me was that I was the best basketball player in the sixth and the seventh grade classes. I was fast, I could dribble with both hands, and I knew from years in the backyard how to be physical. I loved the attention I got from basketball. It somehow made life a little more tolerable and got me some positive attention, which I desperately needed.

At home I hid from the disgrace and shame that I felt inside by staring at a television or playing basketball or any other distraction that was available. My skin just crawled, and I wanted so badly to hurt somebody and release some of the anger and frustration that I had balled up inside of me.

I was an actor without a role. I wanted to have a voice and to finally tell someone what had happened, but in my broken state I didn't know how. What would happen if I said something? Would the family break up? Would I do something that couldn't be undone? My mind was so cluttered with conflicting messages, and now as puberty set in, all of the shame associated with sex and the abuse just made me crazy.

I thought often that I was just crazy. I mean, out of my mind and beyond. I was distracted, disturbed, and despondent. It's difficult to this day to describe the miserable state of mind I was in each and every day, and the only relief was when I was playing or watching sports. It was my great escape, and I knew the alternative to spending time being distracted by sports would have been spent harming someone or something, and that was really counter to who I was or was meant to be.

I believe that the years between sixth grade and the end of my sophomore year in high school were the epitome of hell on earth. There was very little peace in my head, and my actions were maddening attempts to create a new me and control this new creation at the same time. Dr. Frankenstein knows what I mean. During this bleak time I tried various behaviors searching for anything that would fit. I wanted so badly to be good and be like others around me who were getting positive feedback, but I just couldn't control who I was on the inside and, therefore, the behavior that resulted from those feelings.

The dividing line came around the seventh grade when I tasted alcohol and experienced its effects for the first time. If there was hope for me to get the help I needed or some chance for God to intervene, it was lost that day. I was off and running towards the never attainable perfect high. It was the feeling that not only was I in control, and very funny and charming, but also that this feeling would be repeatable anytime I drank.

I had the sense that the real me was somehow available through liquor, and all I needed to do was plug in, drink up, and poof, I would be transformed from the self loathing and destructive mess that I was to a carefree and spontaneous lad with limitless powers and great plans for the future.

I didn't know it at the time, but I was building a prison which would house me for the next twenty-five years. I would not only be the prisoner but also the jailer who held the keys and day in and day out locked me inside with a promise of an ever-fleeting future freedom.

In an amazing twist of irony, I was becoming an alcoholic one messy day or event at a time, and years down the road I would get sober the very same way. Some have suggested over the years that alcohol actually may have saved my life. The real truth is that alcohol may have kept me from suicide, but my career as an alcoholic was certainly no life.

Like a creditor whose complete restitution can never be realized, my addiction showed up every day with its hand out and its need insatiable. I went from miserable and misguided to a budding young addict in a time that felt like a summer afternoon.

I was building a beast that the world occasionally liked but mostly found equal parts idiotic, disruptive, and destructive. I didn't care in the early moments. I had found a way to separate my misery from my reality, even if it was just for a short while.

I had PTSD, and it was great to break the power that hyper vigilance had over me for any amount of time. I looked forward to the next high, and that was my consuming motivation for many years to come. That was my life; the ongoing battle of hyper vigilance and addiction. Not much of a choice but the only two that I knew I had other than suicide, which I often threw into the mix. Not a life really. Not a life at all!

In the years ahead I would trade in dreams and aspirations for numbness. I would start down a path with a goal and an objective and end up in a mind-altered funk. I always wanted to be successful like my older siblings who seemed to have clearly defined plans and who had victories to build on. However, even my small victories were short-lived, and their effects blunted by my ever-enveloping disease. The maddening repetitiveness of addiction and PTSD kept me on a short leash. The end result was just survival. There was insane thinking and there was avoidance and there was fear, and all of those things would leave the stage for a short while when I drank.

Alcohol was a beautiful thing until it turned on me. It turned on me at first in subtle ways, but in time it became the driving force behind my actions and the all encompassing obsession that is alcoholism. It became my constant companion for the next twenty-five years. It started like it does for all alcoholics with that first drink.

Chapter 4

Satan Calls Out to the Boy on the Run

Satan moves in mysterious ways, much like God, though with the opposite goal. This is Satan's time, and he is in haste to gather as many souls as possible. I believe that one of his neatest tricks is having his servants toil away at removing God from our daily lives. The genius is to start in schools and plant the seeds in the young and grow from there. This is a great tragedy for our society.

Another great tragedy for mankind and a victory for evil is that there is very little discussion about evil and Satan, which allows him to push further and further into the fabric of our lives.

As a young boy, I had evil forced upon me. I was given no choice. Evil was tattooed into the marrow of my being, and there was born a new way of thinking and a new way of dealing with the world that I was forced to adopt.

I lost all basic innocence far in advance of adolescence at a time when many children are enjoying freedom from worry and some of the simplest and most enjoyable times of their lives. Those days before puberty and the opposite sex and acne and so many other issues which continue to grow and multiply into adulthood.

One of Satan's most powerful and long lasting tools is addiction of any kind. The earlier that he can introduce mind-altering substances to an individual, the sooner he can stop their maturation process and possess them, and move them towards his way of thinking.

I was ripe for the picking! When I found the relief of

alcohol and then marijuana, I was much more open to Satan's suggestions, and it became much easier to tune out any God-oriented message. You cannot serve two masters.

Satan's messages to budding young addicts include powerful thoughts like: You don't matter. No one really cares about you. You'll feel better when you drink and a host of other intimate messages that combine and take full advantage of a less than fully developed brain and often a child at risk. This creates not only a growing addict but someone who can influence other young minds. It's about multiplication and planting seeds.

In time, Satan would introduce me to other destructive paths, but the most powerful was that he was capitalizing on my addictive nature at a very young and impressionable age. He seized control of my mind, used me as a recruiter, and I followed along on the path to personal destruction and the devaluing of my life. Addiction is the single greatest tool that Satan uses in our society today, in my opinion.

Addiction is the counter to God's truth! It is the anti-truth. I was twelve or thirteen when I found alcohol. I was already predisposed to self loathing and inner turmoil, so I was fertile ground for a life of drugs and alcohol. Addiction is the antithesis of sobriety. The Four Absolutes of Alcoholics Anonymous are: Honesty, Purity, Unselfishness, and Love. The four absolutes of addiction are: dishonesty, impurity, selfishness and hate.

When you start your career as an addict at a young age, and many of us do, we quickly become liars to protect ourselves from parental punishment, and this dishonesty becomes the cornerstone of any addict's life. You will lie to get what you need. You will lie to any level of authority to evade responsibility for your actions. You will lie to yourself to avoid dealing with a disease that is always spreading and impeding normal emotional growth.

I quickly adapted to dishonesty as a way of life. I was already carrying around this deep, dark secret so why not some more deceit? My young mind could not comprehend what I was actually moving towards. I was in the throws of building a new identity, and that was hard. Alcohol made it easier. It reduced the anxiety, and that release led to a freedom and, therefore, a new way of behaving. I was more of a performer than a personality at this point in my life, especially when I drank or drugged.

Satan had a new recruit and a potential officer in his army of young addicts. I was easy prey. Satan's power is immense. I was made impure by another of his recruits. I became selfish in every way when the abuse started. Becoming an addict just furthered that selfishness. All I really cared about was not feeling lousy like I had for the last several years.

The final absolute in Satan's army is hate. I hated how I felt. I hated that someone could hurt me for so long and no one did anything about it. I hated myself more each day. I think it had to do with this complete and utter feeling of frustration. I had no one to talk to. I had no answers myself. I could not find any peace. I was a living and breathing vessel of misery.

I found that my self loathing was distracted by alcohol. The unfortunate part was that it quickly returned when the drinking or drugging started to wear off. It actually became heightened by the impending fear, guilt, and shame of my actions. It was a vicious cycle. It lasted a long time. It took a mighty toll over that time.

Satan's call out to the unsuspecting boy on the run was heard and heeded. I was on the payroll. I would clock in each day, and I would endure the horrible sweat equity I was investing in my new life as an addict. It was the worst job you could have. I was struggling with my abuse history, puberty, and a growing and disabling addiction to alcohol—all at the age of thirteen.

I entered high school barely holding on to my sanity. I was severely distracted and hurting. I could not see any light, and it would get worse over the next two years. I would continue to try to reinvent myself, which often ended in failure and embarrassment. I was a young man with a deep, miserable secret and a growing sense of doom and gloom. I was a long way from God and from peace.

Satan's plan was in full bloom. I was on the road to self-destruction and death. His destructive path was all I could find. His power was in my weakness, and his mightiest weapon was my own self loathing and misery. There was a sense of diminishing light, a waning of hope for the boy on the run.

Chapter 5
Drink, Drank, Drunk

The first time that I tasted alcohol the bond was created, and over the years I would definitely get more than my share. Finding something that took me away from myself was ideal. The idea that it would take me places that would damage me for years was nowhere on the horizon when I slurped down that first beer. The inner pain subsided and a new adventurous self was born.

I used alcohol to numb the pain and be the center of attention. The two uses fit together like hand in glove. In time they needed each other to work. My very first drink was at the age of thirteen when I drank four-and-a-half beers with a straw while my companion got sick after one-and-a-half. The true sign of a budding young drunk is when your buddy is throwing up and you want to know if you can finish his half empty beer. I had a buzz, but the foreshadowing of my tolerance in hindsight is now quite clear.

The alcohol got to the itch that I couldn't quite reach since the abuse started. I was broken into many pieces, and alcohol seemed to pick up the pieces and put them back into the frame of the puzzle. However the pieces were not where they belonged and the image that was created was a bizarre mix of bravado, humor, rage, and charm.

Once I got that booze in my system I came alive, and I was a crazy little bastard who could be dared into doing most anything. Even when I had had enough, I always wanted more. As a minor I would beg, borrow, or steal to get any type of alcohol or marijuana. The psychological cravings had started and, unknown to me at the time, so had the physical want. There just never seemed to be enough. The problem was that most friends got sick if they went too far with mind-altering substances, but not me.

I had a growing tolerance and the stomach to handle the load. It was always the case that time or money or access ran out before my desire was fully quenched. I almost immediately started to have consequences from my consumptive behavior.

At the age of sixteen and without a driver's license, I convinced the best man at my cousin's wedding to give me the keys to the wedding couple's car so that I could go pick up a girlfriend. There was no girlfriend, only the opportunity to drink beer at a friend's house across town.

On the way, I hit a stopped vehicle while making a right hand turn. As it turned out, the other driver was also sixteen and he was driving his father's brand new Cadillac down to the corner store for milk. Needless to say, he was freaked out. When the police and I got the car back to the wedding and let the best man know what had happened, and then my parents found out, well the shit really hit the fan.

The jungle that the abuse made of my mind and the growing addiction as I entered my sophomore year of high school was making quite a mess out of my existence. The obsession to drink and drug was in bloom. It is something only another addict can relate to. Two thirds of the time an addict spends inside his disease obsessing about the next time. That's why I always thought that I could recapture that first feeling of euphoria—my messed up mind told me so.

The longer I drank the more elaborate the obsession became. It's tough to convince yourself that despite all the crap that has happened to you because of your drinking, the next time will be euphoric. It becomes quite the internal ruse.

As a teenager, I just wanted the pain to go away, and I wanted to be that wild and crazy guy who was the life of the party. At the time, I was attending an all boys' Catholic high school. I was playing both football and basketball, but the consistent thought throughout my day was, "when can I use again," so that I didn't have to feel like crap. It's really difficult to concentrate on school or sports when you are obsessing about alcohol and drugs all day long. I was a real mess. My grades sucked, my parents were upset, and the fine Franciscan priests were running out of patience.

An addict always finds like-minded co-patriots. It's usually other hurting young lads and occasionally the downtrodden girls as well. This is a motley group of youths who want to trade in their anger, pain, and, for some, their destructive home lives for a few minutes or hours of escape.

The effect of the supposedly non-addictive drug marijuana is a loss of ambition. It's not an intended result, it's just extremely difficult for regular pot smokers to maintain their attention to detail and their dreams for the future while inhaling a couple of joints at lunchtime.

Towards the end of that school year, the die was cast. I was not going to be invited back for my junior year. I was a free agent, and I was ready to try out the rowdy public school just down the road. My parents however had a different point of view.

My mom was always convinced that no matter what was wrong with me, God was the answer. Even though she was right in the long run, the thing I needed most at this time was for someone to intervene and find out what was wrong with me.

That, unfortunately, never happened and I was forced to attend another parochial high school that had recently gone from all girls to coed and was in need of male students. I was of course disappointed, but I seldom got caught up in vital details. All I needed to know was that the enrollment was going to be four girls to every guy and there were no priests. There was a full scale war going on inside me. I was just an addict with PTSD, and that was plenty for me to handle.

If there was a kid who could use a break, it was me, and the new school turned out to be just such a break. The enrollment consisted of the girls that were already going there, a group of kids from a recently closed parochial school, and the disenfranchised nomads like me. It was an eclectic group to say the very least. We were all just kind of thrown together, and somehow I seemed to fit in. It became time for me to try on a new and improved version of my hybrid personality.

I took my rage to the football field and, even though I was still a clown, I tried hard to stay off the radar screen of the authorities and find some real friends. It sort of worked. I was a starter on both sides of the ball on a pretty bad football team my junior year, and I was the starting point guard on the varsity basketball team. I was funny enough to attract some cute girls and amusing enough to find some other semi-lost boys to form some friendships with. In my very broken world this was progress.

The only thing that created continued problems was that I was still a highly motivated addict, and I was convinced that I could make it all work, and sometimes it did. Unfortunately, there were some very rough times when my addiction beat me down and started to embarrass me.

I really wanted to have a regular date with a nice girl.

The kind where you go to a movie, get some pizza, and make out a little at the end. But my disease told me that unless I got at least a little loaded, I was not going to be able to cope. I felt lousy inside, and I was convinced that as soon as we pulled away from her parents' house, she would start to realize how ugly my insides really were.

Some girls lost interest right away. Some girls probably were insecure themselves and having a few beers wasn't a bad way to start the date. However, there was just one small problem with this plan. I could never stop at just a couple of beers. I got funnier from beers two through eight or so. After eight I got quiet and just wanted to fool around. The problem was again that eight may not be enough, and the girls started to get nervous at this point.

I have to say that I met some of the kindest and most gentle people during my two years at Trinity High School.

I learned later that a good number of people at the school thought I was funny, but they also thought I was crazy and they tried to keep their distance. It hurt to hear, but I could understand why they felt that way. My alcoholism was growing in power, and I was losing control.

I mixed in marijuana and that kept the beer tab down. The issue really became that I didn't know the amount that was needed in order for me to be satisfied, and that scared me a little then and whole lot later. There just was this bottomless hole that I poured into and smoked into, never knowing what the limit was.

The party marched on into my senior year, and on a whim I applied to a couple of colleges along the way and was accepted into two, including Ohio University. As the graduation parties died out and autumn crept into the near future, I decided I would actually show up in Athens, Ohio, and take my act to the next level.

The good news was that I was enjoying some of my life for the first time in ten years. There were moments when I was a star athlete, a funny guy, and a good drinker. That probably described a lot of teenagers in America. Some found a way to drink socially and probably had minimal consequences. Others like me had a problem, and it was only just taking over our lives yet we refused to admit it. I knew on some level that I had a problem with alcohol and drugs. But in that era it was just partying, and the more the merrier, and it was just a warm-up for college, right?

Unknown to me up until my senior year in high school, was that Ohio University was an internationally recognized party school. There was an immediate fit to what I was looking for, and they accepted me, and I accepted them, and off we went into the wild green yonder and Athens, Ohio.

When I think back to my college years now that I have been sober for twelve years, I realize that they were simply lost days and nights and opportunities. It was a chance to really try to discover who I was and to understand my intellectual boundaries. But I was an addict! The words "opportunity" and "addict" are seldom grouped together in an academic setting.

On those rare occasions when I found myself challenged in college, it was overshadowed by my need to choke down the powerful combination of anxiety and depression that encompassed me with alcohol and anything else that would take me away from me.

I found that my roommates where just as distracted by mind-altering substances as I was, especially the young man from Cincinnati, who would leave OU after just one year having really checked out about midway through the first semester. He was a very funny guy with a biblical beard and the most laid-back disposition that God had created.

When I first checked into our four roommate dorm, I found him peeing out the window from the second floor under a giant Jimmy Hendricks poster and as he zipped up, he looked at me and said, "Hey, where are the bathrooms, man?" I was glad I could be there for him. We definitely drank similarly and that was to extreme excess.

I could hold more then my new friend and most other people I came across in college. At one hundred and forty pounds, I was the underdog in most drinking contests. The difference was that I had an insatiable tolerance while many other contestants just liked the idea of winning a drinking game at college.

The ever-growing beast in me was just never really satisfied, and I blew through the stop signs most other men and women at least found to be a warning. The warnings were slurred speech, highly altered motor skills, vomiting, etc. While most found it a badge of honor to pass out, I was just maintaining the addiction that was blossoming in me.

At the beginning of my senior year I was living alone in a tiny efficiency with a hot plate and a tiny refrigerator. I was in the deepest depression of my life, the days passed like seasons, and I was contemplating suicide on a semi-regular basis. Alcohol was my only out. I just could not face the world in this condition most days.

I would sneak out of my hole and like a ghost attend class. Then I would slink back to my hole and try very hard to keep myself distracted and at least remotely sane until darkness came and I could find a loud bar that would allow me to blend into the wallpaper and pour relief on my sickened condition. I was not well.

I wrote my mom one time explaining that I was very depressed. She asked if I was drinking, and I said yes, and she said that I needed to stop and go to church and things would get better. The idea of not drinking was absurd, and I did not know, even after four years, where the Catholic Church was on campus or in Athens in general. I was on my own at least until the holidays. That was a long way off, and I was just barely holding on.

This was when I began reading crime novels for the first time. I inhaled some early Steven King and then found Lawrence Saunders and the Deadly Sins. I would go to class and come home and read. Then I would drink and read, and wake up in the middle of the night after finally passing out and read again. My abuse had begun in the second grade, and my reading skills were definitely disrupted, but I worked through it and had now found another escape besides feeding the addiction beast. These two would be with me for another twenty years as my partners in my attempts to stop the sadness and the loneliness that had taken over my existence.

I was very close to a breakdown in the middle of the semester. The darkness had reached just about every pore of my being and even on the sunniest days of fall I was in deep misery. This is the first time that I found the face of God.

As October crept by and Thanksgiving was still too far away, I woke up in the middle of one night in the deepest and darkest place I had visited to date. I had nothing to drink and nothing to read and nowhere to turn, and so I closed my eyes and I prayed. I begged God for relief and for light and then for rest. I prayed the same "Our Father" over and over again until

I fell into a deep sleep, and for the first time in many days, I found peace.

God had saved my life for the first time, and I kept praying the same prayer each night. He carried me through the next few weeks and into the Thanksgiving break and then into the much longer Christmas break. My life was still very difficult, and my addiction ruled my world, but I had met Christ, and He had offered me His hand and led me out of the darkness and into the light. He knew my pain and despite my addiction and despite my finding no time for Him, He was right there all along waiting patiently for me to fall into His arms.

Once I had recovered enough to do a pretty good imitation of being okay, I forgot to say my prayers and started doing my act without His net again and eventually I would fall. But for the moment, I was renewed by the grace of the Lord. I went back to school early and found a group of girls who had a big house right off campus. They met me and liked the idea of having a man around the house, so they were kind enough to offer me the small room at the end of the hall.

They cooked and cleaned, and they were beautiful, and I was in my version of heaven. I treated them like the three sisters I already had and though a few of the five girls were a little skeptical at first, it turned out to be a wonderful way to finish my senior year at Ohio University.

That summer I delivered Coca-Cola and associated brands of pop in a large truck to supermarkets and beverage stores all over the Cleveland area. It was a great job. I spent the summer working and drinking and ultimately occasionally looking for a job.

I had some moments with the Lord that summer. They were invitations to a relationship with Him that I passed on, but they still stick in my memory many years later. He was never far away, and He wanted to intervene and introduce me to His mercy and love, but I was very busy, and the memories of Him saving my life several months before had drifted far off to the very edges of my radar screen.

But it took only an "Our Father" and He was on the scene and His healing hands were ready to go to work. That's an amazing God. A God who doesn't stop to review your behavior. He just knows that you are in pain, and He wants so badly for you to be introduced to His healing ways that He stands by on call. He knew how far I had fallen, and He never hesitated to find me and lift me up and bring me into the light.

Chapter 6
The Darkest Hours

His eyes were a funky red and yellow as jaundice set in. He was high and only partially there with an occasional blink or spasm. Then he would look you right in the eye . . . it was eerie and, to a stranger, maybe frightening, but not to me . . . not anymore.

His days of making my blood race and my skin crawl were over, and they had been for many years. He was now just a pathetic shell, but in his day he had been a lethal combination of evil and blood relative.

My torture was an inside job, and his unlimited sadism and energy for violence must have been restoked on a regular basis by someone even more advanced in these atrocities than he was. It was like he went away and came back angrier and meaner than when he left. Like his appetite was further developed and his brazen disregard for authority and getting caught were in constant development, being honed by a master of unthinkable things somewhere outside of our home world.

He was like a young actor who read the script and then every pore of his being was transformed into this role as "the spawn of Satan." It was his role of a lifetime and often I was the only other actor on the stage. I took everything he had to dish out and then he would vanish offstage, and I would wait and watch and react with the sole purpose of not being caught on stage alone with him again, if it at all possible.

Though, on this particular evening, the actor was old and his role was reduced to aging drunk and druggie with very little to avert his attention from his overall goal of self destruction and consistent numbness. I watched as he attempted to cajole a cigarette from its soft pack. He raised it shakily to his lips and then, in a movement practiced thousands of times, he found his lighter and sparked the cigarette to life. I lit one of my own and watched him with dulled interest. His hand shook as it made its way to his mouth. The red coal brightened and turned to gray ash and dropped like many before it to the hardwood floor. I am sure that if the ashes would have been landing on something more flammable, I would have left him in the midst of the pyre and would not have looked back.

I was thinking back to the last time I was alone with him. We were playing golf, and the two other guys that we were playing with had left after nine holes and we played on. He was drinking and taking some pills and was getting sloppier as the day went on. I was also drinking heavily that day. At one point he hit his ball sideways into a ravine and went down after it. I followed him and was standing two or three feet above him with a five iron in my hand. I thought it would be so easy to just hit him in the head a few times and then walk away. In that short sequence of time I thought who would know? I could just throw some debris over his body and leave the golf course with outward impunity.

I would normally have more sympathy for someone in this state of slow suicide, but there were too many times that a very small version of me had stared into those empty eyes pleading for an end to his sadistic abuse without relief. As I watched him sitting there, I thought about the times he had cornered me and forced himself into my mouth and I wanted to drive that red hot cigarette into his half opened and yellowing eye.

I thought about the times that he grabbed me by the

throat and slammed my head against a wall and threatened to end my shitty little life if I chose to speak one word of the horrors that were being committed to my person. I thought about taking the large, over-filled, glass ashtray and smashing it repeatedly into his skull until it became mushy.

I thought about the times he stuck his fingers in my ass or as far down my throat as possible, and I contemplated beating him to death with my own two hands and dragging it out and making it last until he begged me to stop and then I would just keep pounding him and dragging his ass around and finding new and more horrible ways to inflict pain until there was nothing left of him or me.

Then and only then would I leave him be. But tonight I sat and observed him as his heart rate slowed, and the cigarette fell to the floor, and he began to snore. I thought that it would be easy to simply stop his breathing for good and then walk away into a life that he no longer inhabited, and at that very moment that seemed to be a workable plan. To banish him to the hell that awaited him. But instead, I picked up the still burning cigarette, crushed it out, and dropped it into the vast pile of butts in the ashtray. I then lifted him up and dropped him onto the couch. I threw his jacket over the top of him, gathered my belongings, grabbed the final beer from the fridge, and left. As I drove in the cold rain, my hands clutched like claws on the wheel, I knew that he deserved less, and I was screwed up for the long haul. But if I kept to the speed limit and kept my eyes on the road, there was a good chance that I would not need an attorney tonight, not for DUI or for homicide, and that felt like a victory, albeit a very minor one.

When losing is all you know any form of, winning can be enjoyable even if it's just for a moment. Considering how few people knew or were willing to admit the truth of what happened in our wonderful home in suburbia, I would have either gotten the chair for killing my own family member or would have been committed for delusional and deviant thoughts and behavior. It was best to keep playing the role I had settled into. The one where I drank enough to forget the pain and the never ending self hatred, and everyone else could get on with their lives. My horror stories were things of the past that should be forgotten and put away for the benefit of the common good. And next Sunday when I would be told in church what a sinner I was and how I must repent, I would be further transcended into that shame ridden and lost soul that I had been for many years. There was no end in sight for this redundant darkness, and the sooner I put this whole thing behind me and walked the walk and talked the talk of a well-adjusted man, the better off everyone else would be.

I Cry Now

I cry now
For me back then
Like suspended emotion
Over several decades
I cry now
To know my severed self
To hold and rock that gentle soul
And offer what was not
I cry now
To better cope with missing him
To help ease our pain
And our lost innocence
I cry now
The tears of rearview mirrors
Seeing again the distraught youth I was
I cry now
To deal with the grief no one shared
I cry now
As I pursue the truth
To lift the boy above the lies
To his rightful place
At the top of the slide
I cry now
As I try to keep him and me safe
Alee from the wind of others' sins
Pointed toward the shore
And a peaceful tomorrow
For a child and a man
So that this boy will cry no more
And this man will weep with joy.

Chapter 7
A Man's Search for Sanity

Even in the quagmire of the addicted mind there are moments of clarity. In 1996, I had one of those moments. My life was a mess, and I woke up one morning feeling like hell and wanting very much to check out of this life. I sure didn't feel like a bout of cold turkey so, in true addictive thinking, I would try to find someone to talk to about what felt like endless misery and pain. I don't remember how I made the connection, but I found a therapist in beautiful Chagrin Falls, Ohio. Sandra had a small cottage behind her residence and that is where we met for the first time on a cold afternoon in January.

I had never been to a therapist so I had no expectations or pre-conceived notions about what I was getting myself into. Sandra had a very calming presence about herself and after I had given her just a thumbnail sketch about my history, she very kindly admitted that she too had been abused and was in recovery, and that was the beginning of the connection for me. I was so used to keeping secrets and talking to family members and friends who just refused to get involved, it was amazing to have someone be so open and vulnerable after knowing me for just fifteen minutes.

Sandra had just one rule that she said was necessary for us to continue. The rule was that I had to be honest to the very best of my abilities. I told her I could do that and we proceeded. To be able to have an open conversation about being molested and abused as a small boy was like a bolt of lightning surging through my entire being. I could feel the eerie and unfamiliar energy flowing back into time and evoking memories and bringing tears into my too-long dry eyes. I bent over and sobbed. Someone was actually listening, and it was true that I was paying them, but at that point in time I just didn't care.

My joy was relatively short-lived due to the next question that Sandra asked: "What is your current usage of alcohol or drugs like?" I stuttered due to the ease at which I could normally lie about that topic, while at the same time hearing the refrain of her only rule bouncing through my ear canals. She had that look in her eye. That look that people get when they know they are being lied to and they are determining how they will handle this knowledge. I said that I drank, but that it was under control at the moment. She asked that I elaborate. I said that my drinking was one of the reasons I was in her office, and she simply said that if she was going to help me, I should consider attending some AA meetings. I had never been to an AA meeting, and I had never really given any consideration to attending meetings. We finished the session without further discussion about my drinking. I drove away excited that I had found a crack in the wall that seemed to stand between me and a new life. I also, for the first time, thought about quitting drinking. But drinking seemed like a very large ship that I was not in control of and, therefore, did not have the power to stop.

I continued to drink, and I continued to see Sandra until one day she said that she could not continue to work with me if I continued to drink. I walked away from hope for the certainty of my oldest and ugliest friend, alcohol. I had given up so much for alcohol, and once again my priorities were numbing the pain instead of working on the source of the pain. It really was no life, but it was the only one I had. For the next few months I tried desperately to control my alcohol until one day when I decided I would do as Sandra had suggested and show up at a detox center and ask for help.

I scheduled an assessment with the intake nurse at Oakview Behavioral Health Center with the potential of staying and detoxing over the weekend. I was assessed and admitted, and I spent the weekend talking to counselors and learning about the disease of alcoholism and having my vitals checked throughout my stay. I completed the weekend and drove away with an outpatient group counseling schedule for the next thirteen weeks. I started attending the group sessions twice a week and made a commitment to the counselor of the group, Terry, that I would try an AA meeting. I did not know it at the time, but Terry would become a very vital part of my initial recovery, and I will always be indebted to him for being very honest with me about the seriousness of the disease I had. He told me there was really just one way to get and stay sober and, in his opinion, it was AA.

I decided that I needed to check out an AA meeting on my own. The real reason was that I wanted the option to leave if I needed to, and I didn't want anyone pressuring me to stay. I parked in front of the church listed in the AA book and stared at the entrance where several people were smoking and greeting people who were entering the meeting. I was scared. The absolute last thing I wanted to do was meet strangers and even worse have strange men shake my hand or, horrors of all horrors, hug me. I lit a cigarette and waited until the last person had left the entrance and then I made my move for the door. I entered a quiet hallway but could hear the rising noise coming from below. I went down the stairs and opened the meeting room door to a scene I will never forget.

Someone was obviously in charge of the concert-like smoke machine, and every type of human being had been invited, and there probably wasn't even any room for me, so I should probably leave. But as I turned, this giant man with a leather Harley Davidson vest and a massive chain attached to his back pocket raised this massive calloused hand and said with a gravelly voice, "Dave . . . alcoholic . . . welcome." That was it. I sat down at a table. One by one each total stranger introduced themselves in similar fashion, I was welcomed to the table, given an ashtray, and the meeting began.

The meeting chairman asked if anyone was new or from out of town and, as if on cue, the entire table turned and looked at me. I made an oath to myself in the car on the way over that I would get there late, keep my mouth shut, and leave as quickly as possible. As if I was having an out of body experience I found myself rising and muttering, "Matt . . . alcoholic." The room exploded into applause, and I was seated.

It wasn't until I was seated that I realized that Dave, the guy I had met earlier, was actually holding on to my elbow. He had actually helped lift me from my chair to introduce myself. Though my AA saga has many twists and turns, that first night was very symbolic of the program itself. It's really just one man lifting another man up and both staying sober one day at a time. Big Dave knew that I was uncomfortable, and even though we didn't move in the same social circles, we certainly had something in common. He knew that his sobriety was based on the principles of AA, and he also knew that by helping me, he was helping himself stay sober for one more day. In its simplest form it is God-focused, God-generated genius.

I continued to go to the group sessions, which were built on the principles of support, accountability, sharing common problems, and getting people to stay active in AA. It was the key to success for several group members, but at one meeting at some point, I stopped listening. I started thinking about drinking earlier in the day, and by the time I left the group I was on my way to the liquor store, and my sobriety of several months was over just like that. My alcoholism was always an obsession first, then the act of drinking, and that was always followed by obsession. It was a cycle that was maddening, but it allowed me to get through the mundane parts of life and return to what I really wanted to do and that was drink. It simply made the madness stop and forced the pain to go away for awhile. I craved the release, and when I finally got that first drink in my hand, my crazy brain began to slow down, and I took my first real breath of the day.

There is zero normalcy in addiction. I was a daily drinker, and any day of the week my plan, which quickly became my obsession, was to drink. Terry from the group called a few times when I didn't show up, but I did not return his call. My old girlfriend, alcohol, was back in town, and I did not have time for the grind of getting sober. I certainly wasn't interested in working the Twelve Steps or going to meetings or any part of that plan. I was back in charge, and even though I was the enemy, I looked a lot like the home team when I got hold of that first drink.

A few weeks later I felt the remorse and pain of heavy use and in a weak moment called Terry. He wanted to know if I was coming to the group that night, and I lied and said I was, and then I asked him why I couldn't seem to stay sober. The phone was quiet for a few seconds and then Terry said, "Well Matt, I don't think you have surrendered yet, and when you do, we will be here for you." I hung up and went to a bar. I was angry. How the hell did he know if I had surrendered or not? How dare he question me and my motives? I would show him.

I would drink myself into a stupor. That would fix him.

A month later, in a new state of despair, I showed up in Terry's doorway. I asked if I could talk to him, and he said sure. I once again told him that I just couldn't stay sober and begged him to help me. He took a moment and then said, "Matt, you need to fully surrender." He said, "You are here," as he put his hands as high as his shoulders, "and you need to be here," as he lifted his arms high over his head. I was blown away. I have no idea why that made so much sense to me, but it did. I asked what I needed to do, and he said, "Ninety meetings in ninety days, and get a sponsor, and show up here for group two nights a week, and start working the steps. That should be a good start."

At that moment in time it sounded like climbing Everest, but what choice did I have. Terry had made it clear that if I was going to bounce back and forth from sobriety to using, he would be inclined to give my seat in the group to someone who was more invested in staying sober. I could get serious or get out. I promised him I would do everything he asked me to. He smiled and said he hoped so. Terry had watched many people come and go, and he was going to pour himself into those who really wanted to stay sober. The part-timers would have to find some other place to waffle. It seemed harsh at the time, but I totally get it now.

Chapter 8
Life on Life's Terms

One of the hardest things to rectify in my life is wondering where God was during the horrors of my abuse. Though I am sure that more will be revealed in time, I believe now that the free will of other human beings leaves many innocents vulnerable. I believe also that the Lord wept during those dark dreary days as he watched sin run rampant and one of his beloved children harmed so deeply.

I spent many years wondering why this happened to me, and in that time I found escape in sin and self destruction. During that time God waited patiently for His beloved son to surrender and accept His healing and in time become a voice and a humble servant for Him on earth. He has held my hand, carried me when necessary, sat beside me when I was too weary to move, and lifted my sagging spirit in times of Satan's many attacks.

As I began to heal, he put a beautiful woman in my life to stand beside me and show me that I am lovable. She accepted me from the very earliest days of our courtship as I was, and stood vigil as I continued to heal and grow into the man God created. We have endured many trials and tribulations in our seven plus years together, and yet today, without a lot of the trappings of this world, we are falling deeper in love — not only with each other — but with the Lord and His enveloping plan for our lives.

When I think of that first day back in 2000 when I threw up my arms in complete surrender to my alcoholism and started to get on my knees every day and ask for His blessings on a new sober day, all the way forward to this journey on a train, His healing touch and His mercy and endless love are more evident with each passing hour. The Lord's love is pure. Every moment of His loving plan is for us to grow closer towards our divine purpose and our just place in heaven.

I have been greatly humbled in this life. I have been in pain so deep that there was almost no hope. I have poisoned myself with mind-altering substances so that I could push the pain away for as long as possible. I have contemplated ending my life to end the pain for good. I have ignored His comfort and counsel. I have tried desperately to amass as much stuff as I could in an attempt to find value in goods. Yet, in the most minute fibers of my being, I knew I belonged to Him, and He was my greatest source of hope, healing, and salvation. His peace is the peace my heart desires. His plan for our days on earth encompasses the talents and experiences we have to offer combined with our willingness to allow His hand to move us at His pace and in His way each day we are here.

We live in a society that in many ways is counter to the Lord's ways. We believe that our value is in what we make of ourselves. We gleam with pride as we are described as "self made men and women."

The message is that we are gods, and if we are a powerful god, we will have great wealth and power, and we will be recognized by other great gods, and we will be applauded for our profits and vision and the castles we have built on earth.

It is really about us and not about the Lord or others. How great a sin it is to ignore our Creator and Savior while we claim our kingdom and exalt our own selfish achievements and accept the lauds that He deserves, while spouting the importance of our existence and erasing in our hearts and souls the importance of His.

In 2002, I accepted a job with Time Warner Media Sales as the Sales Manager in their Akron, Ohio, office. The man I reported to, I'll call him Bob, was a self-proclaimed Christian and was in some ways going to take me under his spiritual wings. I was two years sober and could use some spiritual direction. On the surface it was a perfect opportunity for me.

Upon my arrival, I found that Bob had kept a few very important details from me in the interviewing process. The first was that the man I was replacing was a very disgruntled sixty-two-year-old who was holding the company hostage by threatening to sue them for age discrimination if they even thought about firing him or forcing him into early retirement. The company had treated this guy rather poorly, and they decided that the best thing to do was keep him employed and happy and avoid a lawsuit at all cost. The message to me from the very first day was, "He is your headache now Matt," and they washed their hands of the responsibility and walked away.

Bob led me to believe that he would help me manage this ticking time bomb, and at first I believed him. He would soon also wash his hands of this responsibility and was more than glad to make it mine and mine alone.

The second time bomb that I faced was that the man who was going to replace this older gentleman and who had been with the company for fifteen years was told at the very last minute that I was the new manager and he was not. These two gentlemen now worked directly for me and neither was going to make things easy for me. I was assured by my Christian friend Bob that all was going to be fine and he was going to be in the trenches with me. I would find out very quickly that this was not really going to be the case and that I was really on my own, and life was going to be difficult in my new-found position.

I embraced the difficulties as best I could and started to have an impact on turning a very poorly performing sales group into an award winning team. Bob and I prayed together in his office at lunch. I gave him a crucifix for his office, and we talked about Scripture, and Bob shared his faith with me, and we bonded in our belief in the Lord. Towards the end of 2005, Bob and I hired a young man who seemed down on his luck and in need of an opportunity.

We knew early on that we had made a mistake. This young man had a hard time selling anything and in his frustration he started to upset prospective and current clients to the point that they were calling me and asking me to have their account reassigned. He was wasting their time telling them of his own political views and his opinion on other topics and seldom even responding to their questions and needs.

I spoke with Bob about the issue, and we determined, after reprimanding him on several occasions and coaching him through various techniques, that this individual did not have what it took to be successful and needed to be terminated. I asked Bob if he was completely on board with this action and he assured me he was. I asked this person to join Bob and me in Bob's office one afternoon, and before I could say anything, he and Bob engaged in a dialogue that eventually led to the person keeping his job for an additional two weeks.

I was in shock, and the minute the person left Bob's office I turned to Bob and asked what was going on. He said that he was not very good at firing people and that he did not want to rock the boat. This individual was a very poor employee that had been given multiple opportunities to turn things around, and he was now being given more rope, which was by far a great waste of our time and sent a very bad message to other team members.

The next day this person went to our human resources department and told them that he was bipolar and that I knew this and was harassing him because of this mental condition. I was never informed about the condition, and I had never harassed this individual on any level. I tried very hard to treat him with dignity and respect despite his very poor work record. The situation blew out of control very quickly and within a few days I was summarily fired and walked to the door.

I was stunned. I had been given rave reviews on each quarterly performance assessment with Bob for four consecutive years, and my team had become one of the highest producing divisions in the company. It turns out that despite our relationship and our Christian bond and all of our prayers together, Bob had allowed this dishonest testimony against me to go forward. When he had the opportunity to step up and tell the truth, he stayed seated. He turned his back on me as if he never knew me, and my career has never been the same.

They quickly replaced me with a young man who had been written up several times for harassing female employees, and over the next twelve months the team fell apart and the division has not made its monthly, quarterly, or annual goals since. Bob did not call me after this and did not return my calls for several weeks. His cowardice was amazing and thorough. I finally told my wife that I needed to reach out and forgive this Judas or it would eat me up inside. He finally took my call, and we agreed to meet for lunch. The first words out of his mouth were, "Are you ready to forgive me?" He did not ask for forgiveness or offer any explanation or even ask how I was doing or how my family was doing. He wanted to be absolved, and he wanted to get on with his life. This was a man with very little character who hid behind God as a means to an end, not as a devoted son.

Time Warner even tried to fight my application for unemployment, and when an arbitrator reviewed the evidence, he not only approved the unemployment but thought that Time Warner had gone out of its way to cause harm to an employee in good standing.

I fell into a black hole for several weeks. The destroyed trust issues from my childhood abuse that I had been repairing for over six years took a major hit. It was hard for me to understand why God would put a Christian brother in my path only to have this man betray me and lie about the facts and watch me go down for something I did not do. I was really beaten up and was falling back into old patterns of isolating and pushing the world away at every turn.

We had prepaid for a beach house vacation to South Carolina that was to begin just a week after I was fired. I felt lousy and had lost a lot of confidence, but my loving wife and daughter convinced me that it would do me good to get away, and we had already paid for some of the trip. We decided to go. We were taking my daughter and her two cousins with us, and we had a very fun drive down to Charleston with a week of sun and fun planned.

We were sharing the house with my sister and her family and my mom so the house was full and loud. The second night we were there I was alone in our bedroom when I fell into despair, and despite my anger and my defiance, the Lord brought me a calm that felt so loving. I was in His arms, and I was His beloved son and for fifteen or twenty minutes I knew the power and magnificence of my Master's love! The rest of the vacation had its ups and downs but in the end it was the right move to get away from that heartache and find healing in the southern sun and in the merciful arms of the Lord.

Since that trip God has always met our needs, and though life has not been easy, we have never been hungry, never been without more than we needed, and have always been a prayer away from comfort. I can say that now, but I did not see it in the darkest moments.

One of our toughest battles was the desire for my wife and me to have a child. We had tried for a few years to conceive without success. We then contracted with an adoption agency and began the waiting process for a birth mother to select us. In November of 2009, we were contacted by the agency and informed that a birth mother had chosen our profile and wanted to meet us. She was due very soon and time was of the essence. We met and the connection seemed to be ideal. She was an older woman who already had four children and who just didn't think she could afford another. We were very excited. The birth mother was very open to our involvement in the entire process. She was to give birth around Thanksgiving and we were invited to the hospital the day of the birth.

My wife, daughter, and I got the word that the mother was in labor and off we went to the hospital. A short while later a beautiful boy arrived, and shortly after that we got our first glimpse of his cherubic face. We stayed for awhile and then left with plans to return the next day. We were on cloud nine. We visited and held and adored this little boy that would be the answer to our prayers over the last several years.

We were informed that the child would be taken in by a foster family and that we would be allowed visitation at their

65

home until the necessary legalities were finalized. We spent the Christmas season visiting him and feeding and changing him and falling in love with the child that we would name Luke. Luke began to know our voices and we felt such a close bond. My wife was going to be a mom for the first time and she was glowing with anticipation. My daughter was finally going to have a sibling, something she had wanted her whole life. We were visiting daily and the foster mom was a saint. She had opened her home to many children and her heart was amazing. We were always welcome and always given one-on-one time with Luke.

The holidays came and went and the court date for the finalization of the adoption drew near. The wild card quickly became the estranged father who was living in his parents' basement, unemployed and addicted to pain medications. He was not actively supporting the four children that he had, and there was no sign that he would be active in Luke's life either. We prayed and then we prayed more. The day of the adoption hearing we were joined by other members of our family, and we knelt in adoration in front of the Blessed Eucharist and asked for the Lord to intervene.

Our caseworker from the adoption agency called and informed us that the birth father was not going to sign off on the adoption, and the child would remain for the time being with the foster mother. We were devastated, and in time we learned that Luke was heading home to his birth mother and that he would not be coming home to us. We considered hiring a lawyer but the outlook was not good. The birth mother was capable of at least housing and feeding the child, and without the consent of the father we were really fighting an uphill battle. My poor wife was in mourning, and we wept together. She was angry at God for leading us down this empty path. I was also angry at God, and we both wanted to crawl in a hole and turn the world off completely.

I had tried on several occasions to reach the father prior to the court hearing with no luck. I finally got a return call after the hearing and listened as he told me that no child of his would ever be adopted, and his estranged wife should have known this from the beginning. His pride and his arrogance tasted bitter in my mouth. Regardless of his inability to support and his disinterest in the day-to-day lives of his other four children, no one was going to take his son away from him. The call ended, and a great sadness came over me as I thought about the life that Luke might have in the future. I concluded that he was in God's hands now. I would pray for him, and that would be all that I would be allowed to do.

It's not always a sunny day here on earth. We returned to our daily routine, and in time the pain moved from the surface to our memory. The first Christmas after Luke's birth we thought about Luke being one and we were sad for awhile but moved forward. Life has a way of pulling you ahead even when you don't want to move.

This was a true test of our faith, and we survived the test and put things into perspective and knew at some point that God had a plan for our lives and it may not include another child. My wife and I loved my daughter, Olivia, from my first marriage, deeply, and we appreciate her even more today because she is a wonderful gift from the Lord. We learned to be even more grateful for the things we had, including our faith, and tried to be ready the next time God called our names.

Chapter 9
EMDR — Digging It Up and Moving Forward

In the spring of 2010, my wife mentioned that I could possibly benefit from EMDR Therapy (EMDR Therapy is Eye Movement Desensitization and Reprocessing). It is an integrative psychotherapy approach that has been extensively researched and proven effective for the treatment of trauma (see Appendix at the end of this book for more detailed information). EMDR is a set of standardized protocols that incorporates elements from many different treatment approaches. To date, EMDR Therapy has helped millions of people of all ages relieve many types of psychological stress. I had no idea what EMDR Therapy was, but my wife was attending a seminar in a few weeks and thought she might reach out to a therapist who was supposed to be in attendance. I was struggling with childhood hangover syndrome which is my own term for how I felt.

There was so much pain I was still dragging around from the abuse I had suffered as a little boy that life was kicking my ass day and night. One of my core issues was my inability to stand up to men. It had cost me dearly in the business world, and once again I found myself working for a man who was a liar, a cheat, and a thief, and I was powerless to stop the behavior that was directed at me.

I was hired in January of 2010 as the company was in deep peril. I should have walked away but I needed the job and thought I could help turn the company around. People who were not dealing with full blown PTSD would have taken one whiff of the trouble that they were going to have to deal with and they would have run in the opposite direction.

Two things that seemed to be destroyed during my abuse and the subsequent PTSD and alcoholism were true instincts and self confidence. I really was a wounded guy who needed a job and so off I went.

I was hired as a Sales Director, although at that point there wasn't anyone to direct. I was given an office in another part of the building and was briefly shown how to access some information and some materials about what we sold and was shown the proper way to answer the phone, and the rest was up to me.

Sales dribbled in as our clients and prospects came back from the holidays. The first quarter of any year is usually the most difficult for a sales organization. I was encouraged by the owner of the company to consider rehiring his former General Manager as a salesperson and after a brief interview, and despite my reservations, I did so.

I had quite simply hired a different type of bully. He was a bitter and angry man who liked to stand over my desk and tell me all the things that were wrong with the owner, the company, and in time, me. He spent half of his day complaining and the other half teeing up potential customers for the owner to close the sale on.

Please don't get me wrong, all of the behaviors going on around me were made worse by my inability to deal with stress and to stand up for myself. This had always been the case for me throughout my career.

If you have been in a sales role in your career, you know that the old motto is "under promise and over deliver." Joe, the owner, and Larry, the newly hired salesperson, had worked together for five plus years and their approach, despite my complaints and advice, was to over promise, under deliver, and charge a premium price in the process.

They were shameless when it came to telling prospective clients all of the different services that we offered, when the truth was we had no one on staff to do most of those things.

I had twenty plus years of sales and sales management experience, and I had never witnessed the pure unadulterated aggression and bullshit that these two men offered to clients and prospects each and every day. By May of 2010, I was really overwhelmed by the two alpha males that were panting lies into the phones around me.

I was simply incapable of standing up for myself, and I needed answers before I snapped and did something really crazy.

My wife had gotten the information about Kim, the EMDR Therapist, while she was at the seminar and my first appointment was in the middle of May, 2010. I had done a lot of talk therapy over the years and was pretty comfortable in the therapist setting. I was closing in on ten years of sobriety and I was really ready to take whatever the next steps were to feel better.

Kim was very upbeat and positive, was an abuse survivor herself, and she had benefited greatly from EMDR in the past. She explained that we were going back to revisit the top trauma events that had occurred in my life and we were going to clear them and remove the emotional baggage that I carried with these memories.

My response to any kind of confrontation was flight or I would shut down. I was not very good at the third alternative normally mentioned in PTSD, and that was fight. My fight response was all anger and emotion, and it almost always created more difficulties then it cured. I had learned the hard way that I was not emotionally equipped to fight and win and walk away in a better place. I was hoping and praying that EMDR Therapy would give me that option.

I was very open to anything that would help. I was not completely prepared for the horror show that was going to reveal itself to me as we visited my earliest childhood abuse events. The first thing that struck me was the amazing detail that the memories offered. It was eerie. I was back in the moment, and I could remember drape patterns and the shoes I was wearing and the way I felt before, during, and after that first event.

I was traveling back forty plus years into minutes and hours and days of my life and it was brought to life as if it was captured on film. Like those old eight millimeter cameras with the jerkiness and the bouncing, but the reality was all there. The abuse, the pain, the shock, and eventually the beginning of PTSD and a slow-moving withdrawal from my former state of being into a new numbness and fear that would define me for many years to come.

The hours of therapy went by and the wounds were freshened, and my anger and frustration were revisited on a weekly basis, and I went home and isolated. My wife was there, and she would ask if I wanted to talk and in time I would open up. I would weep and sob and feel tremendous sadness for that little boy who never saw the freight train coming. He was swallowed up and dragged along the tracks for several years and finally left to figure out the rest of his life with the gaping madness positioned in the middle of his heart and soul. The pieces left out in the rail yard were the early foundations of a young innocent boy with promise and hope, and that foundation was ruined and the bricks strewn and the mortar broken and scattered with other unassociated debris.

I spent my days with Jekyll and Jive and my nights trying to make sense of EMDR and how this was all going to help heal me. It is amazing in hindsight that I did not physically harm one or both of the two men I worked with. I am sure they were not living in fear of me but had they known the rage and frustration that forty plus years of ugliness and secrets had created in me, they may have been. I thank God that the white hot rage did not boil over and create more problems then I already had.

As I viewed the horrific abuse, my thoughts were: Why did God let this happen? Why didn't He step in and save me? For awhile as the therapy progressed, I left God on the shelf and tried to stay focused on healing and avoiding the homicidal thoughts that I harbored.

As I have mentioned before, one of the worst side effects of childhood abuse for me was all of the bad decisions I made later in life due to my inability to deal with PTSD and my alcoholism. I wanted desperately to change the course of my life, and regardless of the pain I was feeling, and it was intense, I was not backing down. I was committed to healing these very old wounds and having some peace in my life and being there for my wife and daughter.

As time passed and the intense sessions moved forward, I started to find some relief. The memory was still there but the pain and emotion attached was slowly being removed. Some of the debris was being eased through this seemingly simple therapeutic approach.

As the fall of 2010 began, I was still in the midst of a very difficult work situation. As the business continued to fail, I was asked to not cash my paycheck until the company had the money. This was despite the fact that we had sold plenty for everyone to get paid, however the owner had not been completely honest about his many debts, including an ever growing tax issue with the Federal Government.

At one point, I had nine salary and commission checks that I had held. When I told family and friends my situation, they all said I should get out of there immediately. They were again able to see things through non-PTSD eyes and have boundaries with people in their lives. This was something that I was moving towards, but I was still not able to draw a clear line.

One weekend in October my wife and I had lunch with my brother and his wife. They were astounded that I was holding all of these checks and encouraged me to stop the madness. I was also encouraged by Kim, my therapist, to stand up for myself and call the owner's bluff. I know some of this sounds easy and a little ridiculous, but believe me dealing with PTSD is difficult enough, but having started drinking at the age of twelve, this lethal combination had left me with zero confidence when it came to dealing with male authority figures.

The next week I finally got up the courage to walk out on my employer. I told him that I was going immediately to the bank to cash the nine checks and if he tried to stop payment on the checks, I was going to the Sheriff's office and tell them that he was knowingly writing bad checks.

I had no idea if the bluff about the Sheriff's office was realistic or not but it seemed to have an effect. The owner called my cell and begged me to reconsider. He finally got me to agree to cash two checks immediately and two checks each week until I was caught up.

He was the kind of man that would tell anybody anything as long as it got him through the day. I was uncertain how long he would keep his end of the bargain. Somehow he was able to fulfill his end of the deal throughout the next several weeks. This was due in large part to the fact that I was closing a lot of business and I had become an integral part of making payroll.

I was elated. I had finally been able to have a voice. Since the first day of the abuse I had lost my voice. Here I was forty-four years later and I had finally found it. I could not stop smiling and going over the whole thing in my mind trying to better understand how I did it. I never wanted to lose my voice again.

I had accomplished something that for me and my history was monumental, and I was completely sold that EMDR was the difference. Kim and my loving wife had believed in me, and in the process and the breakthrough that would change my life forever that had finally occurred. I could speak without fear. I could actually have an opinion without feeling afraid of the outcome. I became overwhelmed with the excitement and was not really ready for the next development. A new issue was brewing that would create some extreme havoc in my life and in the lives around me.

I was uncovering secrets that were very ugly about our family, and some of my siblings thought that I was making some of these things up. Others wanted me to keep these things under the rug like they had been for many years.

It created a lot of heartache for me and I am sure for them as well. Having six living siblings created a wide variety of responses. Some ignored the situation, some wanted more information, some doubted the details, and one came immediately to town, heard the news, wept, and left. It complicated my recovery to say the least.

There was one very loud and outrageous verbal fight

that almost turned into a brawl. Though I had found my voice, I wasn't in total control of the volume or the appropriate choices of words just yet. My anger was red and blinding and it sapped my energy, but in the end it was so very freeing.

As I unleashed my venom on my poor questioning sibling, I soared and felt light as a feather. Chains were broken and I was no longer carrying the back breaking weight of shame and guilt and abandonment that I had for so many years. I had some things to say and damn it, somebody was going to listen. I had kept these secrets for over forty years and one of the main reasons I did was to protect the ones that I loved.

Several of my older siblings believed that they were the strong ones. They had been there for me in my struggles and they deserved special mention in their minds. However, I believe today that I was the one who persevered through the greatest of storms. I smiled despite the pain, and I held onto the deadliest of secrets so that no damage would come to my family. In the depths of my own despair, I held my tongue and lived with the misery and kept the secret so that no one else would have to.

The real barometer of the inner strength of a person in my opinion exists not in their physical strength or how they deal with common adversity but how they act when the grief is theirs and theirs alone, and they must bear it and not let it break them no matter what the cost. If great grief has not visited your life, thank God with all of your heart. If an all encompassing grief and pain has been borne upon you and you have endured and not been broken and you have shouldered the burden, I honor you and believe that God has been your total witness.

Jesus was the greatest example of taking the burden upon oneself and being the perfect sacrificial lamb. He went to His death so that you and I could live, and He forgave those who falsely accused Him and beat Him and nailed Him to a tree. His love was greater than anything that His tormentors could offer. His humility and obedience in the face of mortal danger are the single greatest examples of what a hero truly is. I stand in awe of Him and His willingness to die for His friends and enemies.

I completely surrendered to the process of EMDR. I went into the program with a gusto normally reserved for young marines. I was bound and determined to do whatever it took to heal the lifelong burdens of memories almost forty-five years old. I spent nine months in weekly sessions revisiting each significant trauma from my past and clearing them and allowing the young boy in me to finally be free and safe. This young boy had been repressed and ignored for decades. I was stuck right alongside him.

I will tell you that having the ability to take my adult self into a room with my attacker and to show my young self that he was no longer alone was the single greatest feeling amongst all of my breakthrough therapy moments.

I could finally achieve freedom for the child inside me in each of the most horrific episodes of abuse, and that is priceless. It left me in awe, and I wanted to move forward and clear as many memories as possible.

One by one I was removing these layers of misery and doubt from my back. I was losing the self loathing, and the truth was coming to the surface. I could finally protect that small boy image of me and return it in some ways to a more innocent view.

This was truly amazing, and I started to think about all of those other child victims and the adults they had become. I started thinking about how wonderful it would be if they got the same opportunity to clear those horrible memories and move their lives forward.

I thought of a few people that I knew personally whose lives were mired in anger and frustration and who continued to abuse alcohol to numb themselves against the effects of their childhood trauma. I am writing this book for them. To let them know that God is alive and ready to bring them out of the darkness, and I am a living example of that fact.

I have written about my journey and about the many incredible people I have met inside the small churches and halls of AA. I have written about the beauty of God's healing works. I have written about the God sponsored miracles of EMDR. As I move toward completing this book, it is my prayer that through the Lord, it will reach the intended hands and ears and eyes, and I believe His work will be done through me and I will be redeemed through His work.

Chapter 10
Man on the Run to Christ

"He reached down from heaven and rescued me; he drew me out of deep waters" (Psalm 18:16 NLT).

As I trekked across the United Sates on my appointed train ride with Christ, I was closer than I had ever been to a true communion with His wisdom and His desire to heal me. God's mysterious nature was made available to me, a broken boy and man who possessed little in the way of theological training or experience. He certainly will offer you the same access, if you are willing to seek His wisdom and healing.

His instructions for our train ride together were to bring very little other than a Bible and an open spiritual heart. I struggle with the concept of "infinite wisdom" mainly because I am so limited in the wisdom area. His plan for my trip, much like His plan for my recovery and my life, was all-knowing and complete.

He knew that I was prone to distraction and I would need to have a majority of the outside interferences that I was accustomed to removed. That was why the train was His transportation of choice. He knew, and I would quickly find out, that there would be no regular Internet access on the train. He knew that there would be no television access on the train. He also knew that there would be limited phone access, just enough to keep me connected to my wife and daughter and a few business contacts and that was it.

In the twenty-first century, Christ had planned to spend time directly with me, and He offered a very plain and simple place and format. I was moved away from my daily life by an old and somewhat forgotten mode of transportation, a train. I was moved away from the standard, everyday communication systems that constructed my daily life; the Internet, the phone, and the television.

I think back and laugh at how badly I craved a newspaper as we swept across the Great Plains. I tried diligently to get Internet access without success. He had me alone, and it took awhile for me to surrender. My impulsive and easily distracted nature slowed and started to find peace in being alone with my Savior. It was not a natural existence for me, and I continued to feel twinges of involuntary muscle movement towards one of the modern day machines throughout the trip.

The truth is that God offers this type of one-on-one relationship to me all of the time. I believe that He had tried to have this type of away time with me in the past and found it difficult to find a hole in my schedule. I believe that was one of the lessons that God was offering me on this trip: that this was a giant-sized portion of uninterrupted time with my Creator and Lord, it would be an experience that I could draw from for a long time into the future, and more time was always available.

He makes me smile with the many layers of understanding His shared wisdom offers me. He makes me smile when I think of the whole experience and how He had been preparing me for this journey on various levels for many years. The music He was going to play for me on this trip could only be appreciated by a trained ear. One that was open to His voice and His Word. One that was ready for sounds of healing and love. One that was ready to surrender to new music and a new way of listening.

I fought Him and sought distraction and offered partial attention, but in larger and larger chunks of time His message became my primary focus. His messages to me were of the utmost importance for me at this very time in my life. When heeded, they were precise and complete and unforgettable.

The core message that God was delivering over and over to me in different ways was that I was lovable and He loved me. My very name was from Him and the fact that I was on this very journey was proof of His desire to build an ever encompassing relationship with me. I was discovering that I not only had needs, but the truth was that I was need in my totality, and He was the Alpha and the Omega to my need.

A majority of my time with Christ early in my recovery was spent pleading for deliverance from whatever persecution I was feeling at the time. It was often about depression, loneliness, sinfulness, mental confusion, self doubt, faith doubt, parental worries, and many other forms of need.

My fear in recent days had been that though God had certainly delivered me from the treachery of alcohol addiction, I feared He would move on to more pressing issues than mine right in the middle of my battle against the effects of my childhood abuse and the potential healing from my EMDR Therapy. I hoped He wouldn't abandon me. I had to maintain contact with Him or, as they say in AA, I might be left spending too much time with the enemy, who was me.

When I look back now, I smile because God does not abandon us, but quite often we abandon Him. I needed God more then ever as I began to realize that though I was no longer drinking, I was still an addict at the core of my brokenness. Beyond my addictive nature there was the ugly abuse history and all of the negative messages that were programmed into my brain that needed attention.

So much of my current state was tied directly to the abuse. The EMDR Therapy and God's miraculous healing had removed the negative emotional attachments to the abuse, but there was so much more that needed to be cleaned up.

What I came to realize was that this one form of addiction was not the end of my addictive nature. I believe that if I did not get to the root of my issues, I would spend my life moving from one 12-Step Program to another.

I was addicted to escape! The abuse that happened to me occurred when I was so young and completely incapable of understanding and coping with it and its massive fallout. Things in general were just too much for me. I ran away to cope.

There became a white noise in my head that kept me from grasping life's bigger picture. This noise kept me in a strict focus on surviving. That was really the extent of my capabilities. I simply needed to survive. As I got older and realized that there were things that could take me away from the noise, I, of course, was drawn to those activities and quickly became attracted, and eventually addicted, to things that removed the noise.

The noise was removed when I could sleep. It was reduced and eventually removed when I drank or drugged. I knew that if I didn't find things that reduced and removed the noise, I may have a breakdown or my personality may split. There were moments when I felt like I was moving in that direction. These were frightening moments that took me to the very edge of sanity before mercifully ebbing and ending in hard fought sleep or a chemically induced haze.

I was attracted to anything that took me away from dealing with these insurmountable issues. In time, I became addicted to sex, gambling, television, and sugar. I used to think that I was exhibiting sound instincts about who I was and what I was going to face in the days ahead. However, that was not the case.

God knows us intimately and knows our every need. He heals us in His time and in our ability to deal with this new healing experience. I never would have been ready to dive into nine months of intense EMDR Therapy when I was one year sober, for example. I would have been stone deaf to His message on our train ride together back when I was even five years sober, as another example.

The great beauty of staying on a healing course is the opportunity to look back and see how His healing plan was constructed of various puzzle pieces that now seemed to fit together so perfectly. I had been married once before and from that marriage I have a beautiful daughter, Olivia. I was not ready to remarry early in sobriety, but when the time was right, He brought me the perfect woman. The gaps in progress are the times when I turned my back and refused to do the hard work that was necessary or was slow to accept the current healing lesson that I was going through.

Life is all about healing and growing and believing that God is moving you in the healthiest direction. Unfortunately, many people, myself included prior to sobriety, tie God's hands with disbelief. There are many people who in their minds want to be healed of their addictions, but they do not have the necessary faith to get started. The first three steps of recovery in AA have been described as: I can't, God can, and I will let Him.

Sobriety on some level can be obtained and maintained without a belief in God. Healing on the other hand is impossible without Jesus Christ. This may be a point in the book where some people may say "get lost," but it is the true essence of this book's message. I have healed and will continue to heal because I have faith in the Risen Lord! Christ is the embodiment of surrender and healing. He died so we could heal from our sin natures and live eternally. And He was faithful to help me to heal as my search for Him continued.

Chapter 11
Man on a Train

There is a song I love by Jars of Clay entitled "Two Hands" that talks about having two hands: one to pull God closer and one to push Him away, and that had been my relationship up until February of 2011. The company I had worked for after Time Warner had gone out of business in late January, and it seemed like another in a long line of setbacks, but I was determined not to let it get me down. It was in that moment that God stepped forward and called me to His quiet room and instructed me to begin attending daily Mass in the morning. Either my attention span is very short, or God speaks to me in simple ways with the idea that He will give me more when I am ready.

I knew that there was an 8:00 a.m. Mass at our Parish, Holy Family, but the first day and for several days after, I went to the 9:00 a.m. Mass at Saint Mary's Church in the next town over. I found a small group of people who attended Mass in the small chapel every day. I sat up towards the front and watched the priest attentively, and slowly but surely found my self mesmerized by the transformation of the Body and Blood, and I couldn't wait to taste the Lord and feel His power within me.

It was at this Mass that I met Bill, and later we had our two coffee meetings. In hindsight, God was moving me towards my train ride to the Great Northwest, but first he needed me to be in the proper spiritual condition, which for me meant paying attention and being open to His will. The greatest lesson that I learned during this nine weeks of daily Mass and prayer was that God is always asking us and prodding us to a deeper reunion with Him. He craves our time and our attention so that He can help us to reach our divine potential. His love is always available to me if I just open my heart and allow myself to be vulnerable to His will. I have had a sense of free falling into the arms of Christ. In reading the wonderful book that my wife gave me prior to leaving on the train, The Day Christ Died, the author, Jim Bishop, paints a picture of Christ who longs to stay with His friends, who longs, up until His final moment on earth, to be with them and lead them to eternal victory. He clearly loves this band of men who His Father selected and He gathered.

Christ's love for us is greater then any love we have known. It is greater than the love of a spouse or child. I now know that I just need to stop using one hand to push Him away and use both hands to embrace Him and His will for my life. On my journey from Los Angeles to Seattle I met two people whom I am sure God put in my path. It's important for me to remember that there is a far greater chance to meet people whom God has sent my way if I am, in fact, walking towards God and not defiantly in the opposite direction.

The first person I met was a wonderful black woman who turned out to be almost ninety years old, and, as far as I could tell, she was on this train alone and on her way to visit her son in Canada. We talked about a lot of different things and then, as she was getting up to leave, she asked if I knew the origin of my name. I muttered a few things, and she smiled this ancient wise smile and said, "You should spend some time thinking about the origin of your name child," and then she walked away and I never saw her again on that train.

I spent some time shortly after I met Mary Elizabeth looking up my name in the Bible. I knew some of the things that were written there but then this great sense of understanding came over me, and I knew that God wanted me to understand that my name, Matthew, means gift from God, and I should never forget that for the rest of my days. I felt loved at that very moment.

Later that same day, as we pulled into one of the many small stops along the train's route, and as I was going to stretch my legs, an older man with braces on each leg was standing by the door looking a bit confused. I asked if I could help, and he looked at me with tired eyes and said, "I would like a cup of coffee." I said I would be glad to help and asked what he would like to have in the coffee. He said, "Two creams and four sugars," and I was off. We had made no plan as to where we would meet again, and I had no idea where he was sitting. I got the coffee and then began to search every car until I found him in the very back of the train sitting quietly. He saw me coming, and a small smile crossed his weathered face. I stood there while he fixed up his coffee, and then he said, "What do I owe you?" and I said that it was my treat. He thanked me and then slowly closed his eyes and sipped his coffee. I was standing in front of the Lord.

I made a commitment at that point that for the rest of the trip, no matter who asked me for money or help, I would be grateful for what I had and be willing to share it. God was showing His heart to me and showing me that like He demonstrated so often during His time on earth, our greatest love is to be shared with those who need it most.

My journey continued up through southern Oregon and a snowstorm and into the Great Cascade Mountains, and I was often in awe of my Majesty's beautiful design. God was everywhere that I turned. How could I not want to serve this loving King? I continued reading The Day Christ Died, and Jim Bishop's description of the Roman Empire. The Empire lasted for over seven hundred years and was mighty in the many new developments that they brought to the world and especially to the many nations they ruled over. They had the greatest wealth, the greatest army, and the greatest of everything that God put on earth, but they did not have God. They had many other gods that they worshipped, and many thought themselves to be godlike, but they did not have the only God they needed, Christ Himself.

It reminded me of our great nation, The United States of America. Though we have not been around for seven hundred years, we have been blessed with so much and yet seem to be very reluctant to thank and honor the Lord. We find ourselves in very dire circumstances, and our great society is in tremendous need of God's healing powers, but we push Him away. We stand in proud defiance that we will pull ourselves up by our boot straps and persevere. Somehow we have become confused about the role that God has played in our history and the role that our own self reliance should play. I sometimes look around and have a very hard time finding God in our daily lives. I find it amazing that we can't even get to Sunday Mass on time though we get to the movies early. We have lost our way, and still He stands with His arms open wide and welcomes us home whenever we are ready.

As the train wound through flat, frozen, and empty North Dakota and my journey's end was just over a few more horizons, I found myself thinking about what God had in store for me next. I know by now that I am the clay, and He is the artist. His developing plan for my life is beyond my current knowledge, and I must stay open and needy. I am nothing and will become nothing without the Lord. I can hear His voice off in the distance saying, "Matthew John, stay humble young man, for I have work for you to do." (See, the great thing about being the author of this book is that not only do I get to put words in God's mouth, I also can be a young man even when I am not.)

The work that the Lord is referring to is seldom the type of work that a prideful man like me would want on his resume. In my pitiful state, it is usually going out of my way to serve the people that God will put in my path if I am, in fact, on the path to Him. I must be open to His call even if I am going to be inconvenienced or uncomfortable. I must be obedient to His commandments especially when that means I must stop my selfish and sinful behavior before it starts. I must be accepting of His will for my life no matter what the cost. I must remember that true faith is moving at His command, blind as to the final destination, staying alert to new revelations, obedient no matter the loss, and bound to the course, come what may.

Meals on the train are communal, meaning that if you have less then four in your party you will sit with other passengers. It sounded a little strange at first, but it quickly became one of my favorite parts of the experience. The last evening meal I shared with a young married couple, their brand new baby, and the woman's sister. They technically had four but they were gracious enough to break bread with me. The baby was very quiet and beautiful. I was reminded of my own daughter at that age, which was three weeks. The innocence and the complete vulnerability of the child reminded me of an article my wife and I had read recently in the Magnificat, a daily Scripture-based meditation book that I receive each month.

The author was speaking of the final days that Christ spent with His apostles. He says: "Witnessing the countless wondrous works of Jesus Christ brings the apostles to a realization of their own powerlessness. They see in Jesus something that they do not possess in themselves. And they want to possess it. Even more, they want to be totally possessed by the Author of such wonders. Along with the apostles, we come to see that we do not simply have needs; we are need" (Magnificat, Magnificat USA, Yonkers, NY 10702). He goes on to say that as humans we are boundless and expectant, waiting for the Infinite to come close to our life and to claim it.

This is how I felt and what I learned during the trip. God is claiming me and is ready to help me reach my divine potential, and the only thing standing in the way is me. I have a choice each day to surrender to His will or stay stuck in this finite state that most humans accept as their outcome. I hoped as I returned to my daily life that this train ride with the Lord would be the impetus for Him to claim me in full and my surrender would be complete.

On our way through Wisconsin, our path was blocked by a stalled freight train. We learned that there had been a fatality on the tracks. We were told nothing else during the three-hour wait. In less then one day I had witnessed a new life in swaddling clothes and heard of the death of a stranger on the very tracks I was traveling.

I was brought back to the final few chapters of the book The Day Christ Died. The High Priest Caiphus has tried his very best to push the ultimate responsibility of Christ's crucifixion onto Pilate, the Roman Governor. In turn, being the politico that Pilate was, he sent Christ on to Herod, the Jewish King, in a gesture of respect. Herod cannot get Christ to say even one word, and he cannot goad Him into showing any of the miraculous deeds that Herod had heard about, so he sends

Him back to Pilate. Christ spends His entire day after being beaten and spit upon marching from one dishonorable man to the next and never stops this madness or tries to make Himself less vulnerable. He accepts His fate for the love of man.

The earlier chapters of the book spoke of the announcement to Mary of her impending pregnancy and the simple, humble, and completely overlooked birth of Jesus in a barn. The similarities of Christ's birth and death are remarkable. He is born a common citizen, and He dies a common criminal. That is the length that the Lord took to be a completely humble servant to His Father and to His fellow man. That is an uncommon King. That is a man of great character who is the example we need to follow in our walk on earth. This is a God who has nothing but compassion and love for us no matter where we have been or how long we have been gone from His grace.

Our need is complete. Our desire to be vulnerable and completely open to God's will is our commitment to the Risen Lord. In finishing the final hours of the second last leg of my train ride with Christ, I looked back over the one hundred twenty plus hours I have been riding the rails, and I know now things about me and things about how my Lord feels about me that will be treasures for this life and the next. Life as He revealed it, in both a newborn and the fatality on the tracks, is precious and fleeting. I am here to serve Him. There will be temptation and loss, and there will be victories and times of grace, but the end will be death. And I get to decide if I want to be with the Risen Lord in eternity or be left behind in death.

One of the greatest examples that I have from Christ's life is His simplicity. A carpenter's son who spent His youth like any carpenter's son would. His ministry was spent in the company of the outcast, and His band of apostles and disciples were common men who responded to Christ's call. They walked away from their lives and turned their will over to the care of a man they had never met. We are all potential apostles if we choose to give up our adhesions to this world and to follow Him come what may. This simple Man gave up His dignity, His human life, so that we would know Him and need Him and, most importantly, want Him in the center of our lives.

As we clicked and clacked and bumped down the tracks towards Chicago, I was thinking about my loving wife, Victoria, and my loving daughter, Olivia, and my cantankerous, aging, and lovable dog, Buddy, and I realized how immensely blessed that I am. Would I give up my life for them? It's an easy question if I am living a God-directed life. However, back when I was drinking and chasing the fallen one, the answer would not have come so quickly. I was wrapped up in my own misery and did not have a great deal of time to think of others.

What if giving up my life meant being spit upon and humiliated and having my hands and feet nailed to a cross and being stabbed and left to die a common criminal? What would be my answer then? That's a more difficult question that separates this world from the next. Would I really want to leave this life as a common criminal who was hung from a tree in front of my family and friends? Would my pride and my ego stop me from making this final sacrifice for the ones I love? If the answer is no, then I am certainly ready to die for the Lord Jesus Christ. His love for me is far greater than my love for my wife and daughter, so if I am dying for love, I must say yes, right?

Chapter 12
Final Thoughts

In Viktor E. Frankl's book, Man's Search for Meaning, he discovers that the defining difference between those who survived the horrors of the German concentration camp and those who gave up was, in its simplest form, the presence of hope in the survivors. I must be careful here because many who didn't survive did not have any choice at all, but that is a separate issue.

I believe that is the same for me. Somehow through the miseries of abuse, alcoholism, and a life filled with insanity, I kept some small semblance of hope. This hope was in many cases just a faint light kept aglow in a far off corner of my mind. Sometimes it was the wonderful smile of my beloved daughter, Olivia.

I often stayed buoyed by the simple idea that things would change if I could just hold on for one more day, week, month, etc. If faith has a meter, I was very close to flat lining and leaving the monitor all together.

In retrospect, my hope was always tied to God! My fall from a beautiful, innocent child to a ravaged and self-destructive adult felt like a million-mile plummet. God was really the only one capable of reaching those depths, and only through His mercy and grace could I climb back towards the summit. At the bottom of that crevasse, on that surface in the low country of my despair, there was a thin layer between one ounce of hope and hopelessness and a bitter end.

I poked my finger through that thin layer and peered down into the abyss of that bitter end on many occasions and often jerked my head back quickly to avoid finding any comfort in just letting go. The scent of that final free fall would waft upwards and keep me in isolation for days before I found my balance and some semblance of hope and the strength to carry on.

My redemption is an upward walk now. It was a crawl for a long time. The reunification of my child self and my adult self was a great victory that I owe to Christ and two gifted therapists. My child self was trapped in a "fun house" that was clearly beyond his coping abilities. I didn't as much rescue him as I let therapists help me locate him, and Christ lifted him up and put him in my arms. The culmination of this act was captured in one ninety-minute EMDR session that will be a part of my memory for the duration of my life.

The manifestation of hope also took shape in my newfound voice that is evolving and changing as I grow in knowledge of myself and in wisdom handed to me in gentle increments by a loving God.

When I lost my voice as a small boy, I surrendered my opinion and my decisions over to those with voices. They sometimes had my best interest at heart, but most often they had their own best interest at the top their agenda. My voice often came out as shrieks of anger, bursts of sarcasm, and in endless whispers of "help me" that were pointed in the wrong direction and seldom responded to.

When the early facts came out about the young boys who were sexually abused by the Penn State football coach, Jerry Sandusky, my first thought was that the boys had found a group voice to make their stand and be heard and that was good. (Had any one of them tried to fight that battle alone they would probably have been pushed aside, and the needs and interests of the perpetrator and his band of co-conspirators would have won the battle and the war by making it go away.)

When you have no voice, it is hard to believe that anyone with a voice would help you. They haven't been through what you have been through and they don't know what it's like to be so afraid and trust no one. I did try on a few occasions to reach out to an adult and I paid a very dear price.

I believe that many children are abused in many ways in this country every day, and the ones who often are protected are the adult perpetrators and those who may know what's going on but simply turn a blind eye and deaf ear to the cries of the abused. I cringe when I think about what is ahead for the abused child. I pray daily for the children in this country and throughout the world who do not have a voice. They live in fear and in despair and often can't find a way out. Their lives have equal value and meaning to any other person and yet they are reduced and quieted by the evil forces around them.

I want to write a clean and forward moving end to this book but I am caught off guard by a growing need to find a way to give other survivors a voice and a way out. I wrote this book so that in some small way the power of redemption in my life, which has been orchestrated by Jesus Christ, would be a beacon of light for someone still finding only darkness. That goal still remains the same, but I am struck now by a need to say and do more. I hope that this new thought process does not diminish the original purpose of this effort.

For me, there is a regular ebb and flow in my relationship with God. The ebb and flow come from the need for me to do my will and not God's. The seeking of the knowledge of God's will and the conviction to carry it out are the key components for me to living a meaningful life on earth.

In AA the first three steps are about acknowledging our powerlessness over alcohol and the acceptance that God will help us to get and stay sober if we let Him. I entered AA with a God, but not a God of my understanding. The God who I was raised with was a vindictive, powerful God who found me weak and sinful and unworthy. The God I found in AA was a forgiving, loving, and merciful God who was standing at the door with His hand out ready to carry me if necessary from the depths of my despair.

He was at every meeting I attended. He spoke at every meeting. He made coffee and cleaned up afterward and invited me to the next meeting and shook my hand as I was leaving. I didn't realize this at first. I was just going with the flow, and as they say, "fake it 'til you make it" was my philosophy. As I gained more sober days, I started to hear God and then I started to listen more carefully, and in time I realized that God was in the hearts and minds and bodies of each of the members of the program. When it was appropriate, God would put someone I needed in my path and I would progress.

This godly plan is true and has been true throughout my redemption. He has healed people before me so that someone would be there to help me when I arrived. God is alive and thriving in His believers, and the torch has been passed on to me to be there when another survivor is ready. The power of many can do so much when God is at the center of our intentions.

The difference for me at this point in my redemption is that when I finally surrendered to my alcoholic disease my arms where straight up over my head. Now if I am to carry on the Lord's mission, I need to have my hands out in front of me ready to embrace the weariest and most frightened whom I encounter.

This wide embrace shows both my openness to the needs of another, but also it is a consistent reminder of my new life. A life lived out in the open visible to others and representative of the power of Christ's healing touch. When I lived in darkness, I hid from the world. I isolated myself away so that no one would see my scars and my sins. I now know that God can use my scars for good and can heal my sins in preparation for future growth.

Living in the darkness is a life filled with trials and tribulations that offer zero gain or reward, only the option for more misery. Living in the light is also often filled with trials and tribulations, however the gains and rewards are staggering in their depth of joy and knowledge of the brilliance of heaven ahead.

The wisdom that Christ is offering me is anchored in the vitality of the truth. The truth focuses on how I am living and the importance of holding myself accountable on a daily basis and not being afraid to speak the truth when necessary. I am also being taught to love others when I don't want to. Loving certain people in my life will start with forgiveness. This is what some people mean when they say the "road narrows."

If I want to grow closer to Christ, and I do, I must take the narrow path of truth, forgiveness, and loving others no matter what the cost. Christ died for His love of us. He suffered, died, and was buried for our sins. The magnificence of His actions finds its greatest brilliance when He rose from the dead and offered us a new life.

I thought about a new life thousands of times in my past. I ran away from my reality in hopes of finding a new life. I did this physically, mentally, emotionally, and spiritually in various futile attempts at a new existence. Each attempt ended the same way. I was miserably attracted to self destruction, and the chances of a new life were really non-existent. The end of my existence was much more possible than a new one.

That changed when I stopped drinking and started trusting God's AA disciples. It changed when I started spending more time on my knees. My new existence began when I picked up a Bible and began learning about this man, Christ. It continues today when I do those same things, but also when I put Christ and others first.

The promise of a new life has come true. In 2 Corinthians 5:17, it says, "Therefore, if anyone is in Christ, he is a new creation; the old has gone, the new has come!" (NIV). Christ only speaks the truth and always delivers when He is sincerely sought. I am a new man today. I have been brought back from the dead by a loving God and Savior. This book's purpose is just that. To tell anyone who reads it that the Lord Jesus Christ will redeem you and give you a new life if you are willing to do His will and to seek Him. "Love the Lord your God with all your heart and with all your soul and with all your mind and with all your strength" (Mark 12:30, NIV).

I am ending this book now. I have said what I was asked to say by my Savior. I will continue to pray for the children who are abused and who lose their voice and who find darkness at every turn. I understand their pain. I was the boy on the run for too long. I am now the man who is loved and who loves. I am now the man who is working on forgiveness. I am now the man who can reach out to others. I am now the man who can smile and shed tears and feel, and yes, I finally have a voice.

Chapter 13
Epilogue: A Wife's Perspective

Yesterday Matt and I spent time with an engaged couple whom we are mentoring as they prepare for marriage. Spending time ministering to them helped put our own journey into perspective. Matt and I talked a great deal about the importance of God being at the center of their marriage, a companion for their journey ahead. That evening I laid in bed reflecting on Matt's pilgrimage in 2011 and where God has taken us since then. The road hasn't always been straight or even visible; however, no matter what we experienced I have always known that Christ was with us.

Being the spouse of a survivor was never something I thought I would be in my adult life. In my own therapy I had to reflect on how I ended up in this role. I remember having that aha moment in which I realized both my parents had trauma histories of their own. My father was physically and emotionally abused by his father, and my mother was emotionally abused by hers. Loving survivors was a role that I was more comfortable in than I even realized. My father went through a very dark time in his life when I was an adolescent. No matter how hard it got, my mother never abandoned him in his greatest time of need. I had resented her for being weak and staying. Now I see that memory through God's eyes and the significance of the type of love she taught me. My parents have been married now for forty-seven years, and because of them I see the other side of "for worst, for poorer, in sickness, 'til death do us part." They share an amazing bond and love for one another. A synchronicity that can only come from a well seasoned life lived together.

At the end of our second date, Matt and I sat in my driveway as he shared that he was an alcoholic (sober four years then) and sexually abused as a child. I remember not knowing what to say so I simply held his hand. I had no idea then what the journey ahead would become; my naivety kept me moving forward as we eventually prepared for marriage. It wasn't until our honeymoon night that I become aware of what it meant to be the spouse of a survivor, a role that I am still learning about with each stage of our life.

There are many times in our early marriage that I would rather not go back to, days when I felt so alone and lost in the dark abyss of Matt's depression. The aftermath of incest reaches far beyond the initial unholy acts committed against the victim. It can span decades into the future as it swallows up any joy the survivor tries to find in life. It can destroy character, relationships, children, and careers of more than just the survivor. It wants to remain in the dark and can become more evil as the truth is spoken.

Anger is such a natural part of the journey, for all of those involved in the repercussions of incest and sexual abuse. Our anger is separate from that of the survivor. It's tied to the understanding that this person would not be so damaged if this action was never committed against them. Our early marriage would not have been so turbulent had it not been for the residue left behind by incest on the man I loved. I would not have to look into the eyes of the person I love most in life and watch them suffer as they sought relief from the pain they were in. I wouldn't have to pretend that everything was okay, and that my "happily ever after" looked more like, "will he get better?"

My own journey of forgiveness began when I could

ask the question, "Who hurt Matt's offender?" What would cause a teenage boy to brutally attack a younger child? During that time, I was invited to speak to a group of youth ministers about high-risk behaviors and warning signs of teenagers in need. God's hand was all over this because I was scheduled to speak at the parochial school and parish that both Matt and his attacker attended as children. I remember wandering those halls and hearing the ghosts from that time calling to me in a new and more compassionate way. It was in the evening, so the church was closed for the night. I remember asking one of the staff if they could open a door so I could light a candle for the family. In that sanctuary I stood in the darkness with only a small light shining through the door and the faint glow of flickering candles, and I wept for the other lost boy and the story that was never told because of his death. My heart had forgiven him, and I was able to move forward from that sanctuary with a deeper understanding of mercy.

My dearest friend and I are in the process of studying the book of Esther through a Beth Moore Bible series. Beth talks about how a person's destiny is birthed out of their history. That has resonated with me on a deeper level as I have witnessed Matt working through that very process. I have grown to truly respect the person that journeys into their past so that they can fully live in the present. I have learned about the true meaning of love, and the commitment and action it takes to sustain it during difficult times. I have sat beside Matt in his grief, anger, despair, and rebirth. I have watched a miracle happen over time in my own home and in the most sacred places of marriage. I don't blame those who can't stay, I was able to because Matt was not afraid to face his abuse and get help. Beyond that, he put into action what others taught him, and he fought hard to keep Christ at the center. Matt remained in the Spirit of the Lord, and therefore, I was able to remain in the marriage as Matt's companion of healing.

In this journey I have learned how to love unconditionally, grow alongside my spouse, and accept others for where they are. Many individuals have mistakenly thought that it would be easy for me to help Matt because of my clinical background. The wisest words that I had ever heard early on were that I needed to concentrate on being his spouse, and not his therapist. It's always hard for anyone to leave their vocation at the door, but more times than not I was able to do this. It was a relief to know that Matt was working with talented and God-loving therapists who were well educated in the trauma and attachment models theories. Early on in this process, before God led us to Kim, I remember saying to Matt, "If you don't get help, our marriage isn't going to survive." I still laugh about how a couple years into his therapy he came home and said to me, "Vic, if you don't get help, our marriage isn't going to survive." Wow, that was so hard to hear. But because Matt had led the way, it was safe for me to let go of my own dysfunctional ways in which I had coped with his illness so that as a couple we could begin the next stage of healing.

Like Matt, I have been surrounded by the love of the Holy Spirit and the support of some very dear people in my life. Without them, we would never have made it through our own journey into the desert, ever longing for the promise of better days. During this time, Matt and I were also met with other difficult life circumstances. We faced a miscarriage, infertility treatments, infertility, preparation for adoption, loss of the child we were to adopt after we spent three months bonding with him, difficulty in my relationship with his daughter, and multiple job losses for Matt. There were days I felt like a prize fighter in the ring taking blow after blow, all along desperately trying to hold onto my equilibrium so I wouldn't get knocked out. Yet without those times, I would not have recognized what it meant to find the first spring flower poking through the frozen ground, the sweet breeze of mercy from a cool morning breeze, or even the ability to find warmth in the coldest of winter days. In Falling Upward, Richard Rohr talks about how important it is to embrace your shadow, which is made up of both light and dark. When we no longer fear the darkest side of ourselves, but instead embrace it as we learn from it, then we can truly live in the light.

Whenever I am sitting with the loved one of a survivor or survivors, I remind them that what lies ahead is a journey, not a destination. When I stopped trying to rush ahead to "cured" and "recovered," I was able to see what truly mattered. As I write this, Matt and I are still learning how to love one another and growing in our relationship with God. We have begun to taste the first fruits from our early marital experiences together. No matter where you are in your personal journey, may you find God's love and mercy as you travel along the way. Peace and love!

Victoria

Appendix A: Eye Movement Desensitizing and Reprocessing (EMDR)

"Overcoming trauma is a process – a journey. No one travels the journey alone; the Lord is with all of us."

~ Dr. H. Norman Wright

What Is Trauma?

The psychiatric definition of "trauma" is "an event outside normal human experience." Bessel van der Kolk, a leading Posttraumatic Stress Disorder (PTSD) expert defines trauma as an "experience unable to be processed and integrated."

Trauma generally leaves you feeling powerless, helpless, paralyzed. Examples of one-time traumatic events include a bank robbery, a car wreck, or a cancer diagnosis. Ongoing trauma could include combat experience, divorce, and childhood abuse.

Anything can be traumatizing, even minor events such as being teased on the playground, and the same upsetting event may be experienced differently by people and may be stored in the brain differently.

Recent advances in brain science are teaching us much about the way our brains work. Humans are understood to have a physiologically-based information processing system. This can be compared to other body systems, such as digestion in which the body extracts nutrients for health and survival. The information processing system processes the multiple elements of our experiences and stores memories in an accessible and useful form. Memories are linked in networks that contain related thoughts, images, emotions, and sensations. Learning occurs when new associations are forged with material already stored.

However, we know that when a person is very upset, the brain does not process information as it does ordinarily. Consider that our brain has two hemispheres; the left is more logical and the right, more emotional. Experiences that are traumatic for us cause the hemispheres to get out of sync. For example, you may know that what happened to you "is over" but it doesn't feel true. Your logical left-brain, and subjective right-brain are in conflict. Instead of actually "processing" what happened, the upsetting, scary, or traumatic experience remains "stuck" in a state of unfinished incompleteness.

Because the cognitive and sensory aspects of traumatic events are stored "maladaptively," in the nervous system they can still "intrude" into present life and cause symptoms in the present. Traumatic moments may become "frozen in time," and remembering a trauma may feel as bad as going through it the first time because the images, sounds, smells, and feelings haven't changed. Such memories have a lasting negative effect that interferes with the way a person sees the world and the way he or she relates to other people.

What Is Adaptive Information Processing and How Does It Work?

Francine Shapiro developed an Adaptive Information Processing Theory (AIP) to explain and predict the treatment effects seen with Eye Movement Desensitization and Reprocessing (EMDR).

AIP is stimulated by bilateral (left and right) movements

of the body. We are born with the natural instinct to move bilaterally and this is often a rhythmically form of self soothing for many individuals (rocking, walking, swaying, dancing, clapping, tapping, etc). Bilateral stimulation while holding memories in focus seems to allow the brain to release the neural encoding associated with the event and allow other, more adaptive, cognitive process to be linked to the memories. It also seems to trigger the mind to "scroll through" memories and experiences that may be linked together subconsciously and allow these same mature processes to be linked with them, as well.

In other words, instead of the trauma being locked in the nervous system as it was at the time, causing symptoms, the nervous system can finally finish processing what happened, including the images, thoughts, sensations, feelings, in order for it to really know that "it's over." Instead of your body being stuck in a fight, flight, or freeze response, still seeing what happened, feeling what you felt at the time, or thinking about yourself as you did, your system is able to know its over — really over.

The metaphor of a train going down the tracks has been suggested as a way of understanding AIP. As we move forward and process experiences that contribute to the current symptoms, we begin to move towards a more adaptive resolution. As we travel down the tracks, we process the cognitive or sensory–motor material. We pick up newer and more adaptive information as we stop at different train stations. Literally, we are linking adaptive and helpful cognitive and sensory-motor material in existing brain networks, with the track you have been on, the ones that weren't so helpful. In other words, you get what you know logically, to link with how you stored the traumas, as you move forward along the train track. Those emotions, sensations, beliefs, and images that got stored at the time in their state dependent form, are now transformed and stored in more adaptive ways, ways that enable you to feel present, grounded, and no longer hijacked by the events of the past.

What Is EMDR?

EMDR is a therapeutic technique that intentionally harnesses this naturally occurring AIP to assist clients in resolving "unfinished business" from previous traumatic experiences. When doing therapeutic work in this mode, clients are asked to give an image that best represents the trauma that is being worked on. Essentially, it, along with the sounds, feelings, thoughts, and sensations associated with it, is there to "capture" the whole experience. The intention is to help the client access the experience, and all sensory motor aspects of it. Essentially, the client has what is called "dual attention." He or she has one foot in the activated trauma, and one in the present. Meanwhile, the bilateral stimulation activates both hemispheres, to release the trauma's hold on the nervous system.

Successful information processing is thought to occur when a targeted memory is linked with other more adaptive information. Learning then takes place, and the experience is stored with appropriate emotions, able to appropriately guide the person in the future.

EMDR celebrated its 20th year in 2009 and is a researched-based approach to the treatment of trauma. EMDR was developed and initially utilized to help veterans struggling with PTSD. It has been approved by the APA (American

Psychiatric Association) and has been researched for its efficacy in over 20 clinical studies. It has been used successfully on millions of people from all parts of the world, and our United States military has recently spent a lot of money training their mental health clinicians to do this type of therapy.

EMDR is well-suited as both a stand-alone and adjunct therapy, as it is a technique that integrates well with many other forms of psychotherapy. It frequently leads to significant results being achieved in shorter periods of time than approaches that only utilize traditional "talk therapies".

However, it is important to understand that no therapeutic approach is a "cure all" and while EMDR has been found to be useful in a number of clinical applications, it is not typically recommended for those who are having difficulty with reality-testing (psychosis) or severe dissociation.

AIP and EMDR should not be confused with hypnosis or methods for "recovering memories." Unlike hypnosis, EMDR does not involve placing a person in a trance state. Clinical research has shown that AIP and hypnosis activate different regions of the brain. While it is true that when doing EMDR a client may have greater awareness of an aspect of the trauma that was not previously focused on, the goal of the procedure is not to uncover new or repressed memories..

Can Any Clinician Do This Type of Therapy?

While this is an exciting type of treatment that is especially useful for processing trauma experiences, only those who have received proper training and certification should be treating clients with this tool. It is considered an ethical obligation for licensed mental health professionals to only practice within their scope of expertise.

How Is AIP Integrated with EMERGE's Healing of the Mind Model?

One of the legacies of EMERGE founder, minister and psychologist Dr. Richard D. Dobbins was his development of models that assist in understanding the integration of our body, mind, and spirit. In the Healing of the Mind Model, Dr. Dobbins often emphasized that one aspect of healing was to assist people to adopt a more redemptive interpretation of the events of their lives. While they could not change the facts of their lives, they could change the story they told themselves about those facts. Spiritual warfare was often engaged as the enemy of our souls wanted us to accept a version that detracted from the divine potential God had instilled in us. A frequent goal of counseling was to lead clients to a more redemptive understanding of their experiences.

> *"And do not be conformed to this world,*
> *but be transformed by the renewing of*
> *your mind, so that you may prove what*
> *the will of God is, that which is good*
> *and acceptable and perfect."*
> ~ Romans 12:2 (NASB)

EMDR as a therapeutic intervention fits very nicely into this model since they both share a goal of clients being able to see previously distressing events in a new and less disturbing (i.e., more redemptive) manner.

While its underpinnings clearly rest on the solid foundation of empirically validated cognitive behavioral therapy, this approach provides an avenue that permits additional physiological inputs with the ultimate goal of spiritual growth.

Richard Serbin, PhD., Victoria Gutbrod MA, PCC-S

Emerge Counseling Services, Akron, Ohio

References and Resources for a Healing Journey

Jim Bishop, The Day Christ Died (New York, NY: Harper Books, 1957).

Viktor E. Frankl, Man's Search for Meaning (Boston, MA: Beacon Press, 1959).

Thomas a Kempis, The Imitation of Christ (Hollywood, CA: Marcel Rodd Co., 1945).

Peter A. Levine, Waking the Tiger; Healing Trauma (Berkeley, CA: North Atlantic Books, 1997).

Henry J. M. Nouwen, The Dance of Life: Weaving Sorrows and Blessings into One Joyful Step (London, UK: Darton, Longman & Todd Ltd., 2005).

M. Scott Peck, MD, The Road Less Traveled and Beyond; Spiritual Growth in an Age of Anxiety (New York, NY: Touchstone, 1997).

Richard Rohr, Falling Upward: A Spirituality for the Two Halves of Life (San Francisco, CA: Jossey-Bass, 2011).

Richard Rohr, On the Threshold of Transformation: Daily Meditations for Men (Chicago, IL: Loyola Press, 2010). Francine Shapiro, Ph.D., "Eye Movement Desensitization and Reprocessing (EMDR): Basic Principles, Protocols, and Procedures, 2nd Edition" (New York, NY, Guilford Press,

2001). For more information, visit EMDR International Association at: www.emdria.org/.